OECD Reviews of Health Systems: Peru 2017

OECD
BETTER POLICIES FOR BETTER LIVES

Please cite this publication as:
OECD (2017), *OECD Reviews of Health Systems: Peru 2017*, OECD Publishing, Paris.
http://dx.doi.org/10.1787/9789264282735-en

ISBN 978-92-64-28272-8 (print)
ISBN 978-92-64-28273-5 (PDF)

Series: OECD Reviews of Health Systems
ISSN 1990-1429 (print)
ISSN 1990-1410 (online)

Photo credits: Cover © Ministerio de Salud, Peru.

Corrigenda to OECD publications may be found on line at:
www.oecd.org/about/publishing/corrigenda.htm.

Foreword

This is the OECD's first health system review of Peru, and it finds many reasons to commend recent developments in health care delivery. Life expectancy in Peru is now 75.1 years, an improvement of 5.1 years since 2000. Infant and maternal mortality are improving, and are now close to the regional average; infant chronic malnutrition rates have been significantly reduced from 25.4% in 2000 to 14.4% in 2015. Good progress has been made toward universal health coverage (UHC): insurance coverage increased from 37% in 2004 to 83% by the end of April 2017. Institutions such as the dynamic and ambitious *Superintendencia Nacional de Salud* are helping to make sure patient views of their health care are heard and better reflected in service redesign.

Peru's policy goal is to reach full UHC by 2021. If, however, Peru wishes to see its health system as a peer among OECD countries – in terms of accessibility, quality, efficiency and sustainability – issues across multiple fronts now need to be addressed. Exploiting efficiency gains, for example, will be crucial to meet rapidly growing health care demand without putting the public finances on an unsustainable path. Governance and steering of the system from the centre is weak, and arguably weakened further by decentralisation of key competencies to the regions before they were fully equipped to deliver them. Peru's various health care insurer/provider entities also present a major challenge to assuring equal quality and coverage for all Peruvians, whilst gaps in the health system information system – on costs, activities, and outcomes of care – obscure the full picture of health system performance. Most importantly, disparities between different affiliation schemes exist, reinforcing socio-economic and geographic inequalities.

This review identifies the steps that Peru needs to take, in the short and medium term, to build a more accessible, sustainable health system, which is capable of delivering high quality care for all. Going forward Peru needs to underpin reform efforts with a renewed, common vision for the health system. This vision should renew the ambition for reaching universal health coverage, prioritise quality, equity and efficiency, and set out a roadmap that brings sustainable health system improvement for the next decade or more.

Peru should also aim to decrease the fragmentation of the health system, reassessing the current trend towards decentralisation. In some cases – for instance around public health – rolling back functions that have been decentralised too soon may be needed, while in other instances, local and regional authorities will need greater support, tools and funding. To overcome fragmentation a more global vision for integrated services, underpinned by a stronger data infrastructure, will be key. Finally, even with improvements in efficiency, meaningful reform will be extremely challenging without increasing expenditure on health, particularly from public sources.

Acknowledgements

The lead author of this Health System Review was Ian Forde. The other authors of this report were Emily Hewlett, Geronimo Salomon Homer, Ursula Giedion, Lorena Prieto, Tomás Plaza Reneses and Alejandro Posada. The authors wish to thank Francesca Colombo, Mark Pearson and Stefano Scarpetta from the OECD Directorate of Employment, Labour and Social Affairs for their comments and suggestions. Thanks also go to Marlène Mohier and Lucy Hulett for their editorial input and to Duniya Dedeyn for logistical assistance.

The completion of this report would not have been possible without the generous support of Peruvian authorities. This report has benefited from the expertise and material received from many health officials, health professionals, patient groups and other health experts that the OECD review team met during a mission to Peru in September 2015. These included officials from the Directorates for People's Health; for Statistics and Informatics; for Health Promotion; of Epidemiology; for Medicines, Supplies and Drugs; for Environmental Health; of Planning and Budget; and, for Quality in Health in the Ministry of Health; officials from the Seguro Integral de Salud, from EsSalud and from the Sistema Metropolitano de la Solidarida; representatives from the National Superintendency for Health (SUSALUD); National institute for Health; National Institute for Neoplastic Illnesses; National Institute of Child Health; Institute for Health Services Management; Institute for Health Technology Assessment and Research; representatives from the Junta de Usuarios of SUSALUD; the Peruvian Network of Patients and Users; Board of Users of the Peruvian Health Care System; the Forum for Health of the Civil Society; Peruvian Medical Association Peruvian Nursing Association Peruvian Obstetricians Association; Peruvian Association for Quality in Health; Health Practice Council for a Sustainable Health; Peruvian Pharmaceutical-Chemical Association; researchers and academics from the Faculty of Public Health and Administration from the Universidad Peruana Cayetano Heredia; the Medical Faculty of the Universidad Nacional Mayor de San Marcos; the Medical Faculty of the Universidad San Martín de Porres; the School of Government and Public Policy of the Pontificia Universidad Católica del Perú; the School of Government and Public Management of the Universidad

San Martín de Porres; the School of Government and Public Management Universidad; and, the School of Public Management of the Universidad del Pacifico. We particularly thank Dr Midori de Habich, Dr Margarita Petrera Pavone, Dr Janice Seinfeld and Dr Frederico C Guanais de Aguiar for their insights.

The review team is especially thankful to the Minister of Health, both Vice-Ministers and their officials at the Ministry of Health, especially Lic. Rocio Cathia Casildo Canedo, Director General, and Econ. Camilo Alfredo Figueroa Moy, Deputy Director General of the Office for International Technical Cooperation, for their support for this Review and their help with setting up the visit of OECD officials to Peru. This report has benefited from the comments of the Peruvian authorities and experts who reviewed earlier drafts.

Table of contents

Figures

Tables

Acronyms and abbreviations

AN	National Agreement (*Acuerdo Nacional*)
AUS	Universal Health Insurance Law (*Aseguramiento Universal en Salud*)
CHE	Catastrophic Health Expenditure
CPD	Continuing Professional Development
DIGEMID	General Directorate of Medicines, Supplies and Drugs (*Dirección General de Medicamentos, Insumos y Drogas*)
DIRESA	Regional Health Directorates (*Direcciones Regionales de Salud*)
DPT	Diphtheria Polio Tetanus
EPS	Health Provision Entities (*Entidades Prestadoras de Salud)*
EsSalud	Social Health Insurance (*Seguro Social de Salud*)
GDP	Gross Domestic Product
HDI	Human Development Index
HIS	Health Information System
IMF	International Monetary Fund
INEI	National Statistics and Informatics Institute (*Instituto Nacional de Estadística e Informática*)
INS	National Health Institute (*Instituto Nacional de Salud*)
IPRESS	Health Care Providers (*Instituciones Prestadoras de Servicios de Salud*)

LAC	Latin America and the Caribbean
MINSA	Peruvian Ministry of Health (*Ministerio de Salud del Perú*)
NCD	Non-communicable disease
NRUS	New Unique Simplified Regime (*Nuevo Régimen Único Simplificado*)
OGEI	General Office of Statistics and Informatics (*Oficina General de Estadística e Informática*)
OOP	Out-of-pocket
PEAS	Essential Health Insurance Plan (*Plan Esencial de Aseguramiento en Salud*)
PEN	Peruvian Sol
PPP	Public-Private-Partnerships
PPP	Purchasing Power Parity
PpR	Payment by results (*Presupuestos por Resultados*)
PROFAM	*Programa Nacional de Formación en Salud Familiar y Comunitaria*
SCTR	Supplementary Occupational Risk Insurance (*Seguro Complementario de Trabajo de Riesgo*)
SEPS	Superintendence of Health Care Providers (*Superintendencia de Entidades Prestadoras de Salud*)
SERUMS	Rural and Urban Marginal Health Service (*Servicio Rural y Urbano Marginal en Salud*)
SIS	Integral Health Insurance (*Sistema Integral de Salud*)
SPP	Private Pension System (*Sistema Privado de Pensiones*)
SUNAT	National Superintendence of Customs and Tax Administration (*Superintendencia*

	Nacional de Aduanas y Administración Tributaria)
SUSALUD	National Health Superintendence (*Superintendencia Nacional de Salud*)
UHC	Universal Health Coverage
WHO	World Health Organization
YLL	Years of Life Lost

Executive summary

There are many reasons to commend Peru on recent developments in the health system: greatly improved coverage of health care insurance over recent years; outcomes including life expectancy and infant and maternal mortality are improving; and patient views are better reflected. There is substantial room for improvement, however, and the country is now at a crucial time when priorities must be set out and a number of important decisions must be made. If Peru wishes to see its health system as a peer among OECD countries – in terms of outcomes, governance, quality, and information infrastructure – then multiple issues will need to be addressed.

First, a common vision for the future of the Peruvian health system must be established. This vision ought to renew the ambition for reaching universal health coverage, prioritise quality, equity and efficiency, and agree a roadmap that guarantees continuous health system strengthening over the next decade and beyond. In terms of universal enrollment into health insurance, the key challenge is extending insurance to individuals whose incomes are too high to qualify for *Seguro Integral de Salud* (SIS, the government-funded insurer/provider scheme), but who are in informal employment, or are self-employed, and therefore do not qualify for EsSalud coverage (the main insurer/provider scheme for employees). Careful design of regulations and incentives will be needed to ensure that individuals in this group get coverage, drawing from international experience to finish the task and achieve full UHC.

Second, Peru should decrease the fragmentation of the health system. Fragmentation – between vertical subsystems, between national, regional and local competencies, and even between some government agencies – is undermining quality and sustainability. Such fragmentation contributes towards inefficiencies in planning and care delivery, unequal access to care and a somewhat dispersed and disorderly information infrastructure. Without a stronger guiding hand from the centre, this fragmentation is likely to undermine any efforts to achieve universal health care coverage. Frank reassessment of the trend towards decentralization is needed, which may mean rolling back some functions that were decentralised to regional governments before they had the technical capacity to deliver them. In other instances, local and regional authorities may need greater support, and the necessary tools and funding to thrive in a decentralised system.

A more global vision for integrated services will also help overcome differences in access, quality and outcomes across Peru's multiple insurer/provider institutions. Greater use of service-exchange agreements between SIS and EsSalud, for example, would help integrate the system from the patient's point of view – particularly important if people are forced to switch insurer because of a change in their employment status. Other recommendations to overcome fragmentation include more integrated geographical approaches to workforce planning; standard typologies of care providers across subsystems (for instance, categories of primary care provider); and establishing minimum quality standards that apply across the whole system.

Third, Peru must underpin all such reforms with a strong data infrastructure. Whilst Peru currently collects a great deal of information on epidemiological surveillance and health care activities, information on the actual cost of services is weaker, and data on the quality and outcomes of care is weaker still. Linking information on health care needs, activities, costs and outcomes for particular patient groups will be vital to delivering a high-quality, efficient and equitable care and putting the system on a sustainable footing. Peru should combine data from separate insurer/provider entities into a common platform to facilitate performance comparisons and policy planning. In addition, policy makers also need to make better use of information system and better integrate data into the decision making process. This topic is addressed in more detail in the accompanying publication *OECD Reviews of Health Systems: Monitoring Health System Performance in Peru: Data and Statistics*.

Finally, even with improvements in efficiency, meaningful reform will be extremely challenging without committing additional resources to health care delivery. Peru will almost certainly need to increase levels of health spending - especially from public sources. Health spending as a share of GDP is less than the Latin American and the Caribbean average, and too great a proportion of this comes out of pocket, or from other private sources. Even relatively small increases in public spending could still bring significant improvements to health care delivery, if introduced in a targeted, incremental way, while leveraging efficiency and value-for-money. Smarter budgeting and purchasing methods, increasingly linked to outcomes and need rather than merely activity, should accompany any increase in public health care spend.

With sufficient vision and ambition, a national cross-sector effort can address all of these challenges. All players must be driven by an ambition to ensure efficient and effective coverage for all Peruvians regardless of wealth, location or employment status. The goal of UHC and high-performing health care is within reach for Peru, and this Review aims to help Peru to take the next steps to realise that goal.

Assessment and recommendations

The Peruvian population's health needs, and the Peruvian health system, are both young, dynamic, and changing rapidly. Both face complex challenges, where long-standing problems must be confronted alongside emerging concerns. In particular, Peru is experiencing worsening rates of non-communicable diseases – alongside a persistently high rate of infectious disease. The health system, meanwhile, is simultaneously grappling with how to assure basic access – universal health coverage has still not been achieved, for instance – whilst prioritising efficiency and value for money, and improving quality of care.

Encouraging progress toward universal health coverage (UHC) has been made. Insurance coverage has increased in recent years from 37% of the population in 2004 to 83% at the end of April 2017. The Peruvian health care system is nevertheless fragmented into several subsystems, with little integration among them. Disparities between different affiliation schemes exist, leading to socio-economic and geographical inequalities.

Peru's policy goal to reach UHC by 2021 puts pressure on getting more health outcomes with the available resources, especially given the moderate outlook for economic growth in the coming years. This means that the limited resources (financial, personnel, infrastructure and inputs) have to be put to best possible use. Exploiting efficiency gains will be crucial to meet rapidly growing health care demand, without putting the public finances on an unsustainable path. Peru's various insurer/provider subsystems present a major challenge to assuring equal quality and coverage for all Peruvians, especially as governance and steering of the system from the centre is weak, arguably weakened further by decentralisation of key competencies to the regions. Finally, a stronger health system information system – on costs, activities, and outcomes of care – is needed for more effective health system assessment and improvement.

In short, as progress is made towards increased population health system coverage on paper, it will be essential to ensure that accessible and effective coverage for health care services of high quality is also achieved in practice, underpinned a detailed vision for how to promote efficiency, and ensure long-term sustainability.

Developing a renewed vision for the future of the Peruvian health system

Peru's progress in building an effective health care and health insurance systems, that now cover just over four fifths of the population, is commendable. This, and strengthening of the operational capacity of the system, is testament to significant leadership and vision in Peru across the past two decades. Today, however, similar vision and strength of governance are less evident.

The health system faces challenges on several fronts, some of which are fundamental, notably the ongoing need to achieve universal health coverage, fragmentation across vertical subsystems, and navigating a resource-tight context. To build a sustainable, efficient, effective system that serves all Peruvians, a renewed vision for the health system backed by strong central leadership is needed.

Achieving universal health coverage has been a clear focus in Peru for the past 15 years, with some impressive results. Health coverage has increased from 37% in 2004 to 73% in 2015. By April 2017, health coverage was 83.6% according to the *Superintendencia de Salud* (SUSALUD). However, at present an apparent lack of ambition in Peru around finishing the task seems evident: MINSA does not have a long-term strategy for achieving 100% coverage; there are no established targets for increasing health coverage; nor has a timeline for securing 100% coverage been set.

In order to secure health care coverage for the remaining 17% of the Peruvian population, decisive action is needed; at current estimated rates for increasing coverage, a significant proportion of the population will remain uninsured by the end of this decade. Regardless of the approach taken to increase coverage, renewed ambition and strategic vision on the part of the Peruvian authorities is needed. Achieving UHC ought to become a guiding principle of all health policy in Peru. In the midst of an often fragmented health care landscape, the government should seek to make universal coverage a common goal. To achieve this, the Peruvian authorities should gather stakeholders around a commonly agreed Agenda for National Action on Health. This plan would affirm the political ambition for UHC, while setting out a technical roadmap for achieving it.

The key issue is extending health insurance to individuals whose incomes are too high to qualify for *Seguro Integral de Salud* (SIS, the government-funded insurer/provider scheme), but who are in informal employment, or are self-employed, and therefore do not qualify for EsSalud coverage (the main insurer/provider scheme for employees). There are a number of routes open to Peru. One option to achieve UHC would be to expand the scope of SIS. As described in Chapter 1, for example SIS created a "semi-subsidised" regime in 2007, and in 2013 a new attempt to include non-poor populations was made through *SIS Entrepreneurs*, which affiliated independent workers who signed up for the a new, simplified tax regime. Another option would be to develop, or encourage the development of, private health insurance packages that would be attractive to Peruvians who do not qualify for the SIS.

There are some country examples that Peru could follow where UHC has been achieved relatively recently, and relatively rapidly. In particular, Colombia's efforts to reduce the financial burden of health care for households have been particularly successful, as described in the OECD's recent Health System Review of Colombia.

Stronger central governance is needed to reduce fragmentation in the health system

Fragmentation – between vertical subsystems, between national, regional and local competencies, and even between some government agencies – is undermining quality and sustainability in the Peruvian health system. Such fragmentation is contributing towards inefficiencies in planning and care delivery, unequal access to care and a somewhat dispersed and disorderly information infrastructure. Without a stronger guiding hand from the centre, this fragmentation is likely to undermine any efforts to achieve greater health care coverage and equity of quality and access.

There are already some signs that the fragmentation of the system is causing problems for quality of care. The persistence of high infectious disease burden and diminishing vaccination rates are warning signs that regional authorities are not fully competent to provide even basic health care for populations. Critically, resources are fragmented over the different subsystems, creating inequalities for health care access, for instance limiting the development of local health provider networks designed to respond to population needs. Fragmentation of the system also risks undermining the comprehensiveness and efficacy of Peru's quality assurance approaches,by shifting focus to assuring minimum quality standards, rather than driving for continuous quality improvement.

The Ministry of Health (*Ministerio de Salud*, MINSA), as the country's main health authority, is meant to have a global view of the system, including all insurer/provider entities. It must provide strategic management, regulation, and control of the entire system, while guiding provision and financing. Many steps have been taken in strengthening MINSA's stewardship function. For example, MINSA has been reorganised by separating key functions into new vice ministries. Other functions have been moved from MINSA to new agencies. For example, health technology assessments (HTA) and drug purchasing. Nevertheless, the current structure limits MINSA's leadership role in the health system as a whole. For example, EsSalud depends on the Ministry of Labour and is not accountable to MINSA. Similarly, subnational government are not directly accountable to MINSA.

This report proposes strategies to reduce this harmful fragmentation, while maintaining the strengths of a decentralised approach. Such strategies might include: further use of *intercambios* (purchasing agreements) across subsystems to improve access and promote efficiency in provision; an integrated geographical approach to workforce planning; standard typologies of care providers across subsystems (for instance categories of primary care provider); and establishing minimum quality standards that apply across the whole system.

To deliver these results, however, stronger central leadership is needed. Political and administrative decentralisation has taken place very quickly in Peru, meaning that governance skills and capabilities were lost when transferred to the local and regional level. MINSA lost some of its power as the central overseer and decision maker, with some critical functions – for instance vaccination and public health – passed prematurely to regional and local authorities before their competence in these areas had been fully developed.

Moves to re-empower MINSA may engender difficult discussions but, for some core functions, is necessary. Notably, this is particularly advisable regarding quality of care, which is an area that would benefit greatly from partial recentralisation. MINSA should regain the power to set quality frameworks and standards and enforce them, with day-to-day monitoring delegated to an independent arm's length agency, such as SUSALUD.

A robust and interoperable health information system is another fundamental element, as the agency or institution responsible for quality monitoring must be able to perform cross-scheme and cross-geographical comparisons. Whether part of MINSA or not, it is important to count with a national institution that is able to guarantee a high degree of consistency and guidance. Peru could follow the example of Mexico which has been successful at setting up a national agency overseeing health care quality in the country for all insurer/provider entities.

Consequently, some issues could be allowed a greater degree of decentralisation, such as the ability to co-ordinate between SIS and EsSalud. Currently, regions need to gain Lima approval in order to establish these links. Allowing more flexibility and independence to pursue these exchanges would be beneficial for reducing fragmentation both geographically and structurally, and increase efficiency.

Improving coverage and quality will be challenging within current resource levels

Significant injections of additional funding are not the only path to better quality care nevertheless the current level of resources in the Peruvian system will likely render significant expansion of coverage and quality very challenging.

Health care in Peru is less well-resourced than in any OECD country. In 2014 health spending amounted to 5.47% of GDP in Peru, compared to the OECD average of 8.9% and the Latin American and the Caribbean average of 7.11%; per capita, health spending in 2014 was USD PPP 656 in Peru, 5.5 times less than the OECD average of USD PPP 3 866 and less than half the LAC average of USD PPP 1 479. Furthermore, the share of this expenditure coming from public sources was 58.7% in Peru, which also low as compared to the OECD average of 73% (although slightly higher than the LAC average of 56.7%). Public expenditure in health is thus approximately USD 358 per capita, which is almost eight times less than the OECD average of USD 2 854 per capita (although differences in local prices mean that a direct comparison of per capita absolute spending can be misleading).

The impact of limited funding is apparent when taking a broader look at levels of resources in the Peruvian system. Physical access to health services has improved over recent years thanks to investments in infrastructure, but important gaps still remain. The infrastructure investment gap for primary health care is estimated at USD 478 million, for example.

Peru ought to consider two approaches. Firstly, as stressed in Chapter 3, improve efficiency and value-for-money wherever possible, and secondly, give serious consideration to ways that resources flowing into the system could be increased. To make renewed inroads into reducing uninsured populations, and addressing problems with access and quality, Peru will more than likely need to increase levels of health spending. Introduced in a targeted, incremental way, while leveraging efficiency and value-for-money, relatively small increases in resources could still bring significant improvements.

Ensuring access and quality for all Peruvians

Better access and better quality of care should be seen as two sides of the same coin. In a country where nearly one in seven of the population do not have health coverage, access to care remains a major concern. High out-of-pocket payments, geographically uneven distribution of services, and long waits add to the challenges around accessing care. As a result, relatively limited attention has been given to quality of care. The challenges – and the solutions – for improving access and quality are intertwined: vertical subsystems, decentralised governance, and an under-developed health system information infrastructure are all obstacles. A long term strategy for quality and access is needed, with national leadership bringing together a system that is at present hindered by significant fragmentation.

Reaching universal health coverage is the foundation for improving access to care

At present incentives for the uninsured to voluntarily buy health insurance are weak. This translates into high out-of-pocket expenditures to receive care making achievement of effective UHC very difficult. Different options for improving coverage exist, for instance expanding coverage under SIS, or developing insurance packages that are attractive to Peruvians who do not qualify for the SIS as their incomes are too high, but who are in informal employment, or are self-employed, and therefore do not qualify for EsSalud coverage (see Chapter 2).

Another crucial consideration is the minimum benefits package in Peru, the *Plan Esencial de Aseguramiento en Salud* (PEAS). A minimum benefits package constitutes a backbone of any health system: it defines the key health services that are to be guaranteed, delivered, supervised, paid for and financed. In Peru it is time to re-evaluate PEAS, assess its performance, and to find ways to systematically update it. The epidemiology, demand, availability of health technologies, cost and prices are all dynamic aspects that continuously evolve. If these changes are not taken into account a benefits package becomes outdated, losing its utility and, furthermore, legitimacy. If resources to finance the package do not change as demand increases and new technologies introduced, the purchasing power of the package rapidly erodes and effective coverage is no longer guaranteed. Hence, benefits packages need to be accompanied by systematic, periodic and technically robust processes to update them in terms of both scope and financing. OECD countries such as the Netherlands, Israel or Estonia have institutionalised processes to periodically and systematically update their benefits packages.

Addressing financial barriers to accessing care

High out-of-pocket (OOP) spending on health care represents a financial barrier to access. Indeed, OOP expenditure represented 28.6% of total health expenditure in 2014, compared to the OECD average of 19.4% and the Latin

American average of 32.7%. Furthermore, 5% of households could be considered to have incurred catastrophic health expenditure (CHE) in 2012, higher than the 0.73% reported in Costa Rica, although somewhat lower than the 6.4% reported in Chile.

Part of the high OOP can be explained by high levels of cost sharing for services, or payment for services not covered by basic plans. In particular, high OOP spending both for medical consultations and pharmaceuticals are seen in MINSA services. OOP spending in Peru may also be driven by populations who cannot or do not wish to access services under their subsystem for geographical reasons, because of long waits for care, or because perceive they will be better treated in the private sector. Of household spending on health, a reported 40.1% was for the purchase of drugs, 43.3% for the payment of private health services, and 11.6% for public services. This suggests that in addition to possibly routine cost sharing in health coverage plans, Peruvians are seeking out private care because it is easier to access, and/or thought to be of a higher quality. Similarly, the high OOP spend in MINSA could be explained in part by EsSalud insurees seeking care in MINSA facilities because of long waiting times, or perceived poorer services, in EsSalud facilities. This trend underlines the importance of service quality and capacity for ensuring access, as the paragraphs that follow set out. Lastly, of course, high out of pocket spending can be attributed to the approximately 1 in 7 Peruvians who do not have access to pre-paid health insurance.

Better access also depends on improving service capacity and quality

Despite improvements in recent years, infrastructure capacity is another key element limiting access, undermining quality, and putting the sustainability of the system in danger. As described in Chapter 2, high numbers of insured Peruvians are willing to pay for care out-of-pocket for care outside of their insurer's provider network. This strongly suggests that there are shortcomings, either in accessibility of providers in their affiliated network, in quality or perceived quality, or both. For populations covered by both SIS and EsSalud, demand for care is shifting from the formal network private providers and pharmacies, suggesting a lack of confidence in covered services. Peruvians also report being unhappy with the level of accessibility of their health services.

Strengthening the supply and quality of services is a priority therefore. Some promising steps have been taken. MINSA's agreement with regional governments to establish 170 provincial strategic hospitals, 22 regional hospitals and 12 national hospitals by 2021 should, for example, concentrate expertise and quality, but implementation has been slow to date. In looking for further effective ways to increase service capacity, Peru would do well to begin with strengthening primary care provision, and reducing fragmentation across providers.

An important step to improve service capacity and explore potential efficiency gains would be further implementation of *intercambios* (cross-sector purchases of services), giving a greater choice of providers to Peruvians. Initially, SIS could only purchase services from public providers and EsSalud could not buy services from other providers nor sell its services to SIS beneficiaries. Allowing SIS to purchase services from EsSalud providers and vice versa, reduces the health care fragmentation and lead to a more efficient use of the supply of care. Cross-sector purchasing of services is a mechanism for better integrated services for patients; something badly needed in a highly fragmented health system.

Special attention must be paid to the needs of the most vulnerable population, particularly those who are poorer and in remote areas. Health system capacity, specifically in rural and remote areas, is a major concern in Peru. Chapter 2 outlines approaches from Australia, Norway, Germany and France that Peru could consider in looking to strengthen rural and remote health care services.

An expanded workforce, trained in quality, will be critical to achieving effective coverage

In 2013, Peru had 17 physicians and 22 nurses per 10 000 population, reaching the minimum workforce level estimated by the World Health Organisation as being necessary to deliver the health care interventions prioritised by the Millennium Development Goals (MDG). Substantial differences in the distribution across geographic regions, however, remain. Only 10 of Peru's 25 departments have the minimum number of physicians (according to WHO minimum standards).

Peru has taken several important steps to tackle health care work force challenges. A National Health Personnel Register (INFORHUS) was created, for example, in 2013 in order to adequately plan for current and future needs. A National Training Programme in Family and Community Health (PROFAM) was also adopted in 2009, with the goal of strengthening primary care. More recently, MINSA established financial incentives to encourage better productivity and geographic distribution.

The key challenge going forward will be to leverage these policies as step towards achieving a more integrated health care system. Planning must consider the health networks across sectors and regions, and not be limited to the public network. Critically, workforce should also be trained in assuring, monitoring and improving service quality.

Some structural features of the system impede delivery of high quality care

The dual fragmentation of the system, geographically and structurally, a major factor limiting health care quality. The decentralisation process within the Peruvian health care system in theory offered several benefits. Now, however, a return of some core competencies to central authorities, and stronger levers to push regions towards good performance, are both needed.

One clear example of an area where core centralised functions is advisable concerns public health. Strong health protection and prevention efforts need to be led from the centre, and complemented by local capacity. The quality of infectious diseases care is very poor in some areas, with the central authorities unable to impose adequate standards. Peru may furthermore need to consider ways of compelling regions to fulfil certain functions, for instance ruling that a certain percentage of regional health funds are spent on preventive health activities, for example. In Mexico, a strong centralised institution has led to a more positive impact of health prevention activities across all levels of government. A unit belonging to the Mexican Ministry of Health is in charge of epidemiological surveillance, community oriented public health interventions, vaccination, dengue fever controls, protection against outbreaks and natural disasters. The success of this approach suggests that Peru could improve health outcomes by returning some competencies to MINSA.

Certain key quality assurance functions also need to be strengthened, and would likely benefit from being entrusted to a strong, independent, national agency. The DIGESA (environmental health) and DIGEMID (pharmaceuticals and medical devices) agencies, which have experienced a degree of decentralisation, appear to be performing well. Although a model of accreditation is directed by SUSALUD exists, for example, no national accreditation programme for hospitals is in place (although this is currently being reviewed). What is missing is an assurance approach that covers service providers across all subsystems, nationwide.

As well as strengthening quality assurance, Peru should look to introduce ways to focus attention on quality improvement. Given Peru's highly fragmented health system, a unifying national standards framework for quality could, as it has done in Australia, have a positive effect on quality improvement. Australia's standards are high-level and quite broad (for instance covering governance framework, communication between clinicians, safe handling of blood products and medication safety), but crucially have been agreed by stakeholders across Australia. A move towards using voluntary accreditation for hospitals and eventually other providers would be another welcome quality improvement step. Such a move would be particularly effective if greater competition could be introduced between subsystems, and if patients could more easily choose between service providers on the basis of public signs of quality. For this to be effective, the *intercambios* or another form of service exchange would need to be more operational. Here, Portugal offers a good model to follow; the Portuguese national accreditation programme is a key strategy to promote quality in hospital outcome of care, wherein the accreditation framework follows key priorities identified in the National Health Programme, including patient-centred care, sustainability and equity.

Service user and patient participation has evolved successfully and should be further encouraged

In the area of patient engagement and education there is much to commend in Peru, and in particular longstanding engagement of patient rights groups. The *Superintendencia Nacional de Salud* (SUSALUD), the main agency responsible for patient engagement and handling complaints, is a dynamic and ambitious institution. SUSALUD created a regular survey, ENSUSALUD, through in-hospital representatives and health literacy initiatives. SUSALUD's *Juntas de Usuarios* in particular are effective in generating patient exchange, and there is a good case for broader roll out of the *Juntas de Usuarios*, which should be celebrated as an example of good practice in deepening engagement with patients.

There are still areas where Peru could learn from OECD countries, however, such as Denmark. There, groups have been formulating increasingly sophisticated understandings of patient needs, and lobbying for change in a system-wide way, with focus including appropriate models of care, or financial access. Furthermore, SUSALUD is expected to become further decentralised in the near future, and it is uncertain how this will affect its capacity to exercise its mandate. Compared to the rest of heavily decentralised and fragmented system, SUSALUD is a national institution that breaks the norm since it is concerned with all patients regardless of affiliation. It is crucial that the influence of SUSALUD and its capacity to reflect the views of patients – including to national level actors, and political actors – be maintained and even strengthened.

Peru should focus on using health system information to drive quality of care

Indicators of provider performance can point to sites of best practice from which peers can learn. Indicators can also be used to drive quality improvement, shining a light on weaker performers and pushing them to improve, supporting the system to move in the right direction over time. In expanding the health data infrastructure, Peru should look to begin collecting and reporting indicators of health care quality in line with the OECD's internationally comparable "Health Care Quality Indicators". While the ENAHO health survey does include some of these indicators (notably screening and some vaccinations), many others are missing, or collected by only part of the system. Ideally these indicators should be collected and reported broken down across subsystems, by region, and also at an aggregate national level. Reporting on these key indicators of health care quality would be illuminating in terms of comparing performance to OECD countries, but perhaps more importantly, it could help shine a light on variation between regions, and between subsystems, in Peru.

The Peruvian health information system has made progress during recent years in regards to some type of data, such as on activities and human resources (INFORHUS). Data on quality of care remains poorly developed however, and addressing this should be a priority. In particular, more data and outcomes should be collected and processed. Following the recommended list of OECD quality indicators, would be a good starting point.

The fragmentation of the health system is one of the factors limiting the capacity of the information system. Peru should combine data from separate insurer/provider entities into a common platform to facilitate comparisons and policy planning. The involvement of a national agency (possibly as part of MINSA) could further support collection, processing and use of information. In addition, policy makers also need to make better use of information system and better integrate data into the decision making process. There is currently a disconnection between research and decision making, with many key policies not supported by empirical research.

It is also important to focus on user-friendly data presentation, and promote accessibility of data. Indicators of need, activity, outcomes and cost should be made more visible and understandable in order to be useful for patients. SUSALUD already performs this role of data sharing with patients but it could benefit from having access to a larger number of indicators.

Finally, a recent OECD Council recommendation highlights the importance of building public trust and confidence in health data and strong safeguards that govern the transparent use and transmission of personal health. This involves bringing down barriers to the utilisation and sharing of data but also ensuring that the public is fully involved in decisions about data collection and use. Monitoring of adequate standards in privacy and utilisation should be a top priority. The OECD recommends that Peru addresses these aspects in its further development of the health information system. Detailed analysis and recommendations to strengthen Peru's health system information infrastructure can be found in the accompanying publication *OECD Reviews of Health Systems: Monitoring Health System Performance in Peru: Data and Statistics*.

Increasing the efficiency and sustainability of the Peruvian health system

Focusing on efficiency and sustainability for the health system is essential for ensuring that Peruvians have access to high quality health care in the decades to come, but is also fundamental for effectively using resources today. Achieving universal health coverage under current financial restraints implies that a focus on improving quality of care needs go hand-in-hand with promoting efficiency.

Efficiency gains could be achieved by filling resource gaps and addressing budgeting methods. In terms of sustainability, it is important that reforms are both politically *and* financially sustainable. In particular, health system reform must last through changes in government and through times of economic instability.

Improving access and health care coverage should be seen as a sustainability and efficiency issue

Assuring effective health care coverage, and access to appropriate care can prevent escalation of illness and ultimately higher costs – either for the health system, or for individuals and their households, or both. By way of example, increases in infectious disease rates including dengue and chikungunya in some regions are extremely worrying, and are likely to be more costly to treat than to prevent. Taking a still broader perspective, inadequate access to health care undermines health and wellbeing, and therefore the productive potential, of society.

The number of health insurance affiliates has been growing steadily for the last 15 years. This is clearly welcome, but does bring challenges with respect to sustainability. Increased coverage without the necessary growth in resources means that the system, faced with growing demand, appears under strain. There is a trend for individuals to seek care from providers not included in their insurer's network. This means that, to some extent, increased coverage is not translating into adequate access or financial protection.

The beginning of this chapter stressed that improving coverage and quality will be challenging within current resource levels. This is most certainly true, but beyond this there is a need to focus services towards coverage that promotes sustainability – for instance, preventive health and primary care – and maximise the efficient use of existing resources.

Increasing efficiency through strategic purchasing and use of health technology assessment

One of the most positive changes in Peru's public management capability in the health sector was the introduction of the centralised purchasing for drugs. MINSA has been centrally purchasing drugs for the last decade; in a way that shows good inter-scheme co-operation and that has been successful in reducing prices. But, this strategic approach has stopped evolving and needs to be further developed. The reverse auction process, for example, should be reviewed to allow for more competition. At present, the auction starting price (from which providers seek to under-bid each other) is based on the previous year's "winning" and therefore lowest price. This limits the ability of manufacturers to bid a competitive price, and has meant that competition no longer exists for close to 20% of the drugs, and many providers have stopped offering these drugs altogether.

There are also efficiency gains to be made by expanding the list of medicines manufacturers beyond the one provided by the World Health Organization. In particular, WHO's list of prequalified medicines, does not include countries that have their own production lines.[1] For example, Brazil produces several vaccines at low cost. Expanding the list of approved manufacturers could help to further reduce prices. It is important to stress, though, that the expansion of this list should guarantee quality.

Similarly, Peru needs to review the methodology used to prepare the List of Drugs for National Purchase including high cost drugs for less frequent treatments. Adjustments and updates to this list currently happen in an ad hoc fashion. The list should be updated periodically and systematically and processes to do so should be institutionalised. Chile, for example, mandates that its benefits package AUGE must be updated regularly, while Colombia stipulates that its benefits package POS is updated every year and that process has to rest on evidence and participatory processes.

There is also an opportunity to provide assistance to regional governments in the planning of their drug procurement. Systems to anticipate critical stock levels, and warn regional governments and MINSA of the risk of falling below this level, would be welcome for example. This would reduce the need of emergency procurements at higher costs, improving efficiency.

MINSA also has the opportunity to build on the various promising initiatives in health technology assessment (HTA). MINSA should co-ordinate and reinforce the existing agencies are starting to carry out HTA. The *Instituto de Evaluación de Tecnologías en Salud e Invesitgación* (IETSI) in EsSalud or the INS and DIGEMID in MINSA, for example, could co-ordinate to determine the coverage and price of high cost drugs.

Using solid evidence and HTA to determine what is and what is not to be financed by health systems has become common practice in most OECD and many Latin American countries. For example, Colombia has constituted an independent HTA agency, IETS (*Instituto de Evaluación de Tecnologías Sanitarias*) which is now systematically and routinely providing recommendations to the Ministry of Health on the benefits and costs of health technologies. Likewise, in Uruguay, a National High Cost Drug Fund, FNR (*Fondo Nacional de Recursos*) evaluates new drugs to determine whether they should be provided by it universal health system. One of the best known HTA institutes is United Kingdom's NICE (National Institute for Health and Care Excellence) which appraises health technologies and produces recommendations on whether they should or should not be provided by the national health system. It is important that processes are systematic, technically robust, participatory, independent and established at the national level.

SIS needs to operate as an effective insurer

A fundamental element of efficiency reforms should be revision of SIS's competencies. The success of SIS in the future depends on strengthening its capacity to operate as a true insurer. SIS currently does not have the tools to adequately manage either population health or institutional financial risks, and it is being held back by that, in particular from a sustainability perspective.

The first issue is that SIS lacks the necessary autonomy to make key decisions, which are now responsibility of MINSA (and also of the Ministry of Finance in some cases). SIS currently negotiates its budget with the Ministry of Finance on a daily basis, instead of being able to collect its own financial resources as other countries in the region do, such as Colombia. Although the Law states that SIS should receive funding based on its number of affiliates, this is not currently being implemented.

Critically, the allocation of resources for SIS is generally made through political decisions rather than technical assessment. This happens both because of the lack of integration and quality of information systems, but also due to the sometimes excessive weight political agendas have on policy making. The growth of SIS's enrolled population has also often been decided politically, without formal modelling of likely impacts on sustainability and efficiency. Expansions of SIS's affiliated population is a step forward in terms of achieving UHC, but when the needs and challenges of SIS are not taken into account, may not translate into effective coverage in practice.

In order to facilitate the reform of SIS and turn it into an effective insurer, first, Peru ought to ensure that the SIS budget is based on actuarial studies. Second, SIS should implement a risk management model through better capacity to analyse health care needs and activity. Third, SIS should increase its ability to strategically purchase without necessarily always going through the intermediation of the Ministry of Finance. Finally, SIS, MINSA and the regional governments would do well to work together in carry out a study of the actual cost of services, to better ensure that regional resource allocations match service obligations.

Presupuestos por Resultados (PpR) is a positive measure to improve budget allocation, but it needs to be further integrated

Accurate budgeting and financing remain as a big challenge for Peru, which has traditionally used historic budgets to decide on resource allocation. The Ministry of Economics and Finance (MEF) base their budgets on previous year's allocation, the projected availability of resources and negotiations with MINSA and local authorities. This does little to fight overspending and tends to perpetuate resource gaps and inequities. With the exception of EsSalud, all public health institutions compete for MEF funds.

Promisingly, more innovative forms of budgeting have been introduced in recent decades, such as payments per results (*Presupuestos por Resultados*, or PpR) in 2007, which has been introduced as part of the budgeting system at all government levels. Under this new approach, budgeting switched from budget lines (human resources, goods and services, etc.) to an intervention-based, costing and production goals method. The PpR is defined as "a public management strategy that links resource allocation to products and measurable results for the population". Its methodology includes a careful choice of interventions, a clear definition of the expected results and a commitment from participating institutions to achieve them. It is intended to establish public spending accountability and mechanisms for data generation.

By selecting key interventions based on health priorities, PpRs are meant to improve allocative efficiency and performance. One example is the childhood nutrition programme, which targeted interventions such as growth and development checks and iron supplementation. Implementation of the PpR was associated with a reduction in the prevalence malnutrition in children under five years of age of 9%, between 2009 to 2014.

However, while switching towards PpR improves how budgets are established and allocated, it does not address the question of the amount of financial resources that are needed for the health sector. In particular, because PpRs are established for specific priorities, they do not provide a systematic view of budgeting, and operate independently of financing schemes.

Overall, then, PpRs needs to be better integrated with other funding mechanisms to maximise their potential positive impact. A key requisite in order to maximise the value of PpRs is to increase the planning and managing capacity of the institutions involved in the health system, something that Peru is lacking. This is fundamental in order to guarantee insurers can adequately handle the responsibility of managing their own funds independently across different programmes. Being able to allocate resources flexibly and with a strategic vision can be the key to achieving efficiency gains which are deemed so necessary.

Conclusions

There are many reasons to commend Peru on recent developments in the health system: greatly improved health care insurance coverage over recent years; outcomes including life expectancy and infant and maternal mortality are improving; patient views are better reflected. However, there is room for improvement and the country is now at a crucial time, when priorities must be set out and a number of important decisions must be made. If Peru wishes to see its health system as a peer among OECD countries – in terms of outcomes, governance, quality, and information infrastructure – then now is the time to act.

First, a common vision for the future of the Peruvian health system must be established. This vision ought to renew the ambition for reaching universal health coverage, prioritise quality, equity and efficiency, and agree a roadmap that brings sustainable health system improvement for the next decade or more. Secondly, Peru should aim to decrease the fragmentation of the health system. This will likely include a reassessment of the current trend towards decentralisation, in some cases even rolling back functions that may have been decentralised too soon. In other instances, local and regional authorities may need greater support, and the necessary tools and funding to thrive in a decentralised system. Subscheme fragmentation is another priority area to address, including driven by a more global vision for integrated services. Third, Peru would be wise to underpin any such reforms with a strong data infrastructure. The importance of health system information is highlighted in this review, in respect to understanding and improving quality, efficiency and sustainability. The accompanying publication, *OECD Reviews of Health Systems: Monitoring Health System Performance in Peru: Data and Statistics*, addresses challenges and opportunities in the Peruvian health information system in greater depth, with particular focus on national health accounts. Finally, even with improvements in efficiency, meaningful reform will be extremely challenging without increased committing increased resources, and increasing expenditure on health.

With sufficient vision and ambition, together with a true multi-stakeholder effort to address the existing challenges, the goal of UHC is within reach for Peru. All players must be driven by an ambition to ensure efficient and effective coverage for all Peruvians regardless of wealth, location or employment status.

Key recommendations to strengthen health system performance in Peru

Peru is on the right track to achieve UHC and a health system that is sustainable and works for everyone. However, in order to increase the number of insured and maximise efficiency, quality and access for those affiliated, a number of policy reforms are advised. The top priority recommendations are:

To promote access to high quality care and achieve universal health coverage, Peru should:

- Renew and strengthen the national ambition for achieving Universal Health Coverage, gathering stakeholders around a commonly agreed Agenda for National Action on Health, which would affirm the political ambition for UHC, while setting out a technical roadmap to achieve it.
- Take action to reduce unhelpful fragmentation between subsystems and regions, through greater use of *intercambios* (purchasing agreements) across subsystems, integrating geographical planning, and standardising typologies of care providers.
- Establish minimum quality standards that apply across the whole system, so that Peruvians can expect the same standards of care from any provider, anywhere in the country.
- Carve out a stronger role for central leadership, re-empowering MINSA in key domains including setting and enforcing quality standards, and public health functions.
- Consider whether the current level of resources in the Peruvian system will allow for increases in coverage, as well as gains in quality of care.
- Ensure that any increases in health spending are introduced in a targeted, incremental way, while leveraging efficiency and value-for-money.
- Re-evaluate the PEAS minimum benefits package, to assess whether this package still provides adequate coverage for Peruvians, and whether the PEAS is adequately funded.
- Further invest in the health care workforce, to ensure a more even supply across geographic regions, and to ensure that all workers receive training in monitoring and improving service quality.

Key recommendations to strengthen health system performance in Peru *(cont.)*

To become a data-driven health system, putting people at the centre, Peru should:

- Build on the strength of SUSALUD and the ENSUSALUD survey in reflecting patient satisfaction and patient views. SUSALUD and other patient advocacy approaches should be embedded nation-wide and developed further to increase the patient-centredness of care.
- Collect indicators of health care quality – using the OECD HCQI indicators as a blueprint – benchmarking and publishing them nationally, regionally, and broken down by subsystem. Information exchanges between sub-schemes should be promoted further.
- Focus on user-friendly presentation of data on health care needs, activities, outcomes and costs. In particular, data on quality and outcomes should be made more accessible for patients, policy makers, and health professionals.
- Bring down barriers to the utilisation and sharing of data, but also ensure that the public is fully involved in the process, with patient consent and confidentiality prioritised.

To take a more strategic approach to funding, budgeting, and purchasing, Peru should:

- Develop more sustainable and consistent approaches to budgeting and resource allocation, moving away from budgets based on historical spending, and towards an intervention-based, costing and production goals based budgeting method.
- Embed strategic purchasing through reinforced Health Technology Assessment; HTA efforts carried out by a range of different agencies could be co-ordinated by MINSA to avoid duplication and determine the coverage and price of high cost drugs and other technologies.
- Take a more strategic approach to purchasing in the health system, in particular expanding the list of approved drug producers, reviewing the approved pharmaceuticals purchase list, and take a more centralised approach to planning to anticipate necessary drugs stocks.
- Give more independence to SIS, so that it can operate as a true insurer; SIS needs more decision making power, especially over the availability of resources, approaches to growing the insured population, and strategic purchasing.

Note

1. WHO Prequalification of Medicines Programme (PQP) helps "ensure that medicines supplied by procurement agencies meet acceptable standards of quality, safety and efficacy" (WHO-Prequal, 2016). The process for manufacturers to include their products in this list is led by WHO. For more information, see: http://www.who.int/mediacentre/factsheets/fs278/en/.

Chapter 1

Health and health care in Peru

This chapter describes the context within which the Peruvian health care operates. It begins by summarising the main demographic, socio-economic and epidemiologic trends in Peru. Key achievements towards achieving universal health coverage are discussed, as well as remaining challenges.

The structure of the Peruvian health care system is described, with a particular focus on the key actors within the government-funded health care sector. The chapter also describes the systems to raise and distribute financial resources, and closes by analysing information systems underpinning health care delivery in Peru.

Introduction

Peru has achieved substantial progress towards universal health coverage (UHC), as measured by the proportion of the population formally enrolled into a health insurance scheme. Health insurance coverage increased from 37% in 2004 to 83% in April 2017. Nevertheless, 17% of the population still does not have any form of health insurance, demonstrating that distance that remains before fully achieving UHC in Peru.

This chapter first presents the socio-economic context in Peru, as well as the main health care needs in the country. Later, it presents the structure of the Peruvian health care system, describing the governance and financing of health care services and highlighting key challenges that the health care system must be able to respond to effectively. Lastly, this chapter describes information systems underpinning health care delivery.

1.1. Socio-economic context and health care needs in Peru

Despite a sustained positive macroeconomic performance that has almost halved poverty levels in the last decade, around one in every four Peruvians is still poor. Inequality is relatively low for the region, but considerably high in comparison to OECD countries. This section sets out the socio-economic context of the Peruvian health care system and it explores the health care needs that the health system must address.

Peru's geography and demographic characteristics present a challenging context for the health system

Peru is the third largest country in Latin America and is extremely diverse, both geographically and in socio-economic terms. The country is divided into 25 departments, bordering Ecuador and Colombia to the north, Brazil in the east and Bolivia and Chile in the south, with the Pacific Ocean to the west (Figure 1.1). The Andes mountain chain passes through Peru which, together with the Amazonas jungle in the north-east, creates a geographically complex setting. In 2014, Peru had nearly 31 million inhabitants (World Bank, 2016), most living along the Pacific coast, with fewer in the mountain ranges and rainforests. The indigenous population in Peru accounts for approximately 30% of the population (INEI, 2014), although an alternative estimate by the National Institute for the Development of Andean, Amazon and Afroperuvian Peoples (INDEPA) is was only 13% in 2015. Urbanisation is happening rapidly: 78% of the population lived in urban areas in 2014, projected to increase to 82% by 2025.

Figure 1.1. The departments of Peru

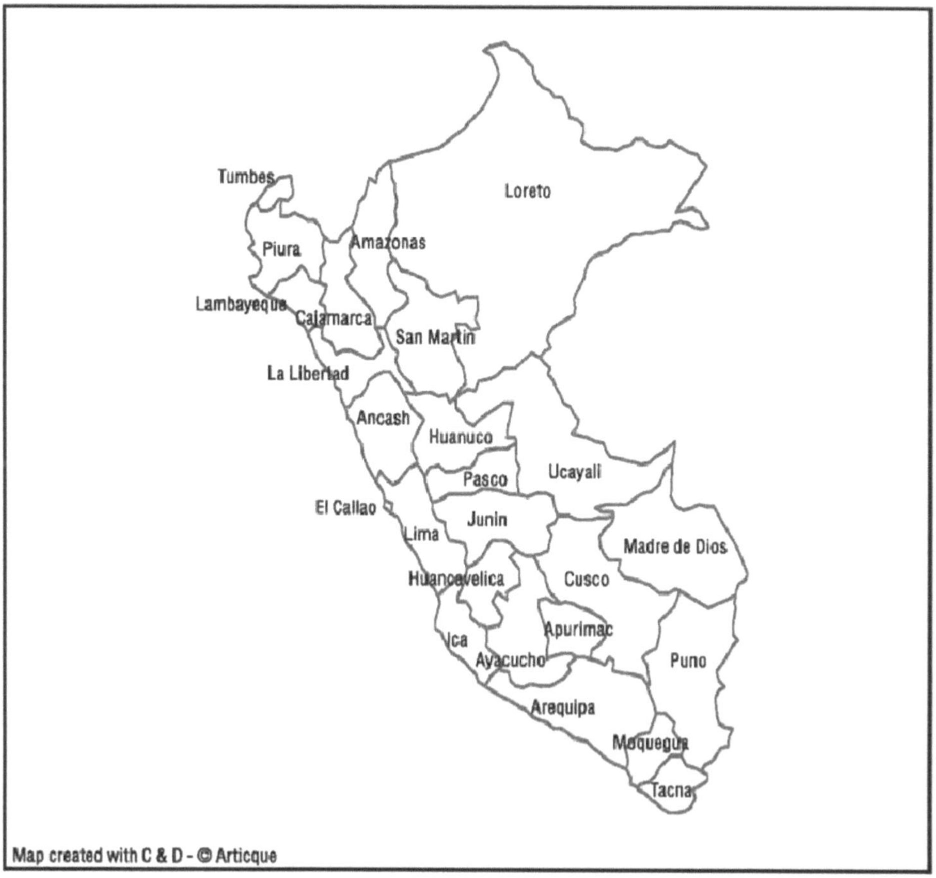

Source: OECD (2015), *Multi-dimensional Review of Peru: Volume 1. Initial Assessment*, OECD Development Pathways, OECD Publishing, Paris, http://dx.doi.org/10.1787/9789264243279-en.

Life expectancy in Peru reached 75.1 years in 2016. Successes in tackling poverty and inequality have contributed to more rapid increases in life expectancy in Peru over the past ten years than in OECD countries. While life expectancy increased by 3.4 years on average across OECD countries between 2000 and 2015 (rising from 77.1 years to 80.5 years), it increased in Peru by 5.1 years (up from 70.0 years in 2000). Even more remarkably, life expectancy in Peru increased from 53.5 years in 1970 to 75.1 years in 2016, a 21.6 year increase (the biggest increase among comparable Latin American countries along with Bolivia); as compared to an average of 10.4 year increase among the OECD countries during the same time period (Figure 1.2). But despite the reduced gap to the OECD average, longevity in Peru is still lower than in all OECD member countries.

Mortality rates decreased from 545 deaths per 100 000 inhabitants in 2005 to 530 per 100 000 inhabitants in 2013; and the global fertility rate in Peru was 2.42 children per woman, down from 2.69 in 2005 (World Bank, 2016). The Peruvian population is relatively young in comparison to OECD countries, but the country is undergoing a demographic transition. As a result of decreases in mortality and fertility rates, along with increases in life expectancy, the Peruvian population is rapidly ageing, meaning that the number of working-age people for every person over 65 will drop sharply in the coming years. In short, Peru's shifting population pyramid resembles that of OECD countries, with a narrowing base and expanding numbers of older adults (Figure 1.3). This development inevitably impacts on the health of the population and puts pressure on the health care system.

Figure 1.2. Life expectancy at birth among OECD and Latin American countries, 1970 and 2015 (or nearest year)

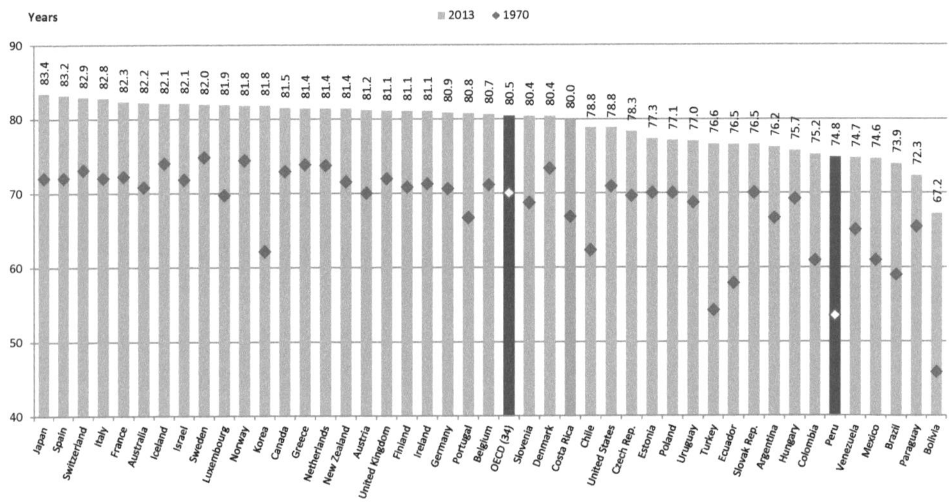

Source: OECD Health Statistics 2016, http://dx.doi.org/10.1787/health-data-en and World Bank (2016), "World Development Indicators", retrieved from: http://databank.worldbank.org/data/reports.aspx?source=world-development-indicators.

Figure 1.3. Population pyramid in Peru by sex and age for 2000, 2015 and projections 2030

Population, %

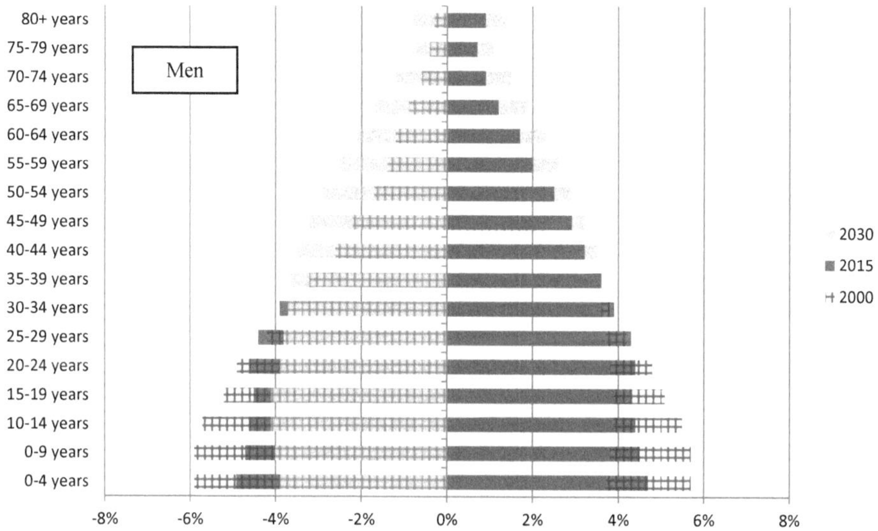

Source: United Nations Department on Economic and Social Affairs, Population Division. World Population Prospects: The 2015 Revision, https://populationpyramid.net/peru/2015/.

Economic growth has been rapid, but poverty and inequality remain high

Following the 2009 global financial crisis, the Peruvian economy grew at annual rates of over 5% until 2013. Following a decline in commodities' prices, growth decelerated to 2.4% in 2014, which represents the lowest growth rate since 2009. The International Monetary Fund however projects 4.0% growth in 2020.

Broadly positive economic performance in Peru has enabled strong growth in employment rates and income, leading to significantly reduced poverty rates. Between 2004 and 2015, poverty rates more than halved, from about 59% to 22 % of the population (Figure 1.4; INEI, 2016). There was also a dramatic decline in the share of the population living below the extreme poverty line, from 16% to 4% in the last decade.

Despite these achievements, Peru still displays high level of poverty in international comparison, far above the OECD average of 10%. The indigenous population faces particularly high poverty rates, with wealth gap between the indigenous population and non-indigenous communities persisting due to a lack of access to education and public services.

Figure 1.4. Evolution of poverty and extreme poverty in Peru, 2004-15

As percentage of total population

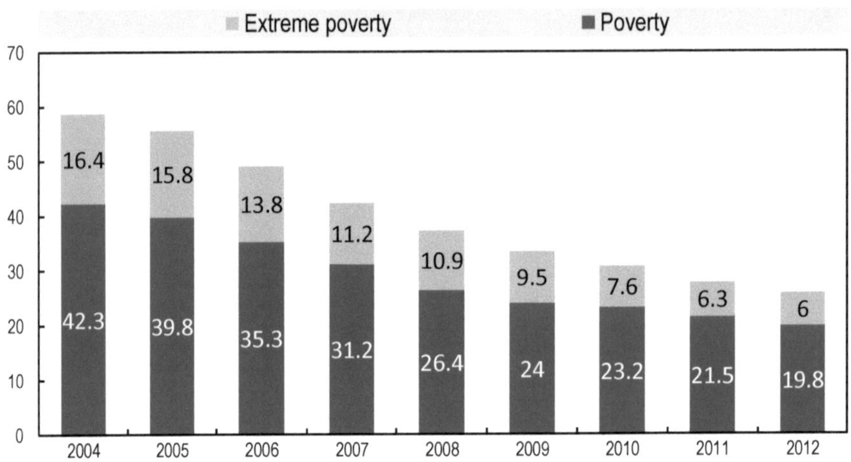

Source: INEI (2016), *Encuesta Nacional de Hogares, Instituto Nacional de Estadística e Informática.*

The absolute level of inequality in Peru is relatively low as compared to other Latin American countries; but it is higher than in most OECD countries. Inequality, as measured by the Gini coefficient,[1] has declined from 0.49 in 2004 to 0.44 in 2013 (INEI, 2014). This indicator is still far above the OECD average of 0.31 in 2013, although lower than in Chile and Mexico, 0.50 and 0.47 respectively (Figure 1.5). The annual average income of the top 10% of Peruvians was 26 times higher than that of the bottom 10% in 2009 (UNDP, 2009), as compared to an average ratio of 9 across OECD countries (OECD, 2016).

Figure 1.5. Income inequality in OECD countries and Peru

Gini coefficient

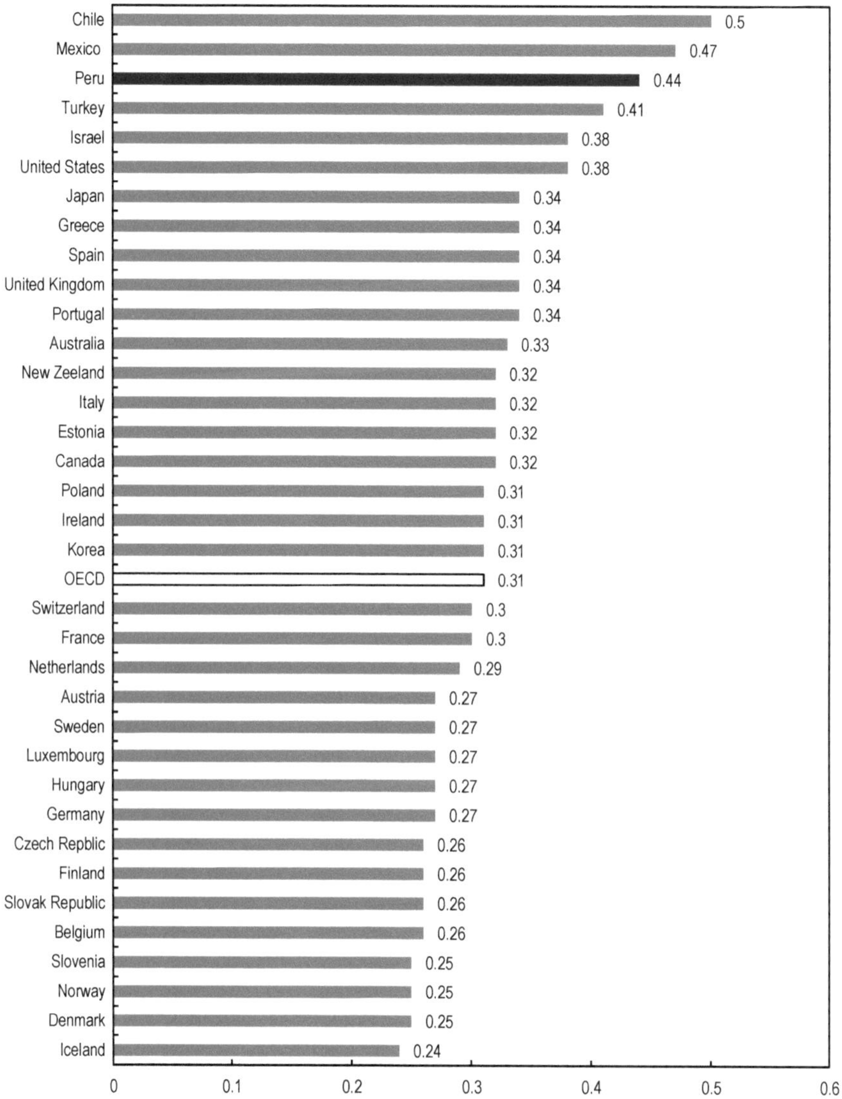

Source: OECD (2014), *Society at a Glance 2014: OECD Social Indicators*, OECD Publishing, Paris, http://dx.doi.org/10.1787/soc_glance-2014-en; World Bank (2016), "World Development Indicators", retrieved from: http://databank.worldbank.org/data/reports.aspx?source=world-development-indicators.

Improvements in aggregate inequality mask some important geographical differences: as of 2013, the Gini coefficient in the coastal region was 0.40, while in the highland and rainforest regions it reached 0.47 (INEI, 2014). While GDP per capita in Peru as a whole was USD PPP 12 042 in 2014, Apurímac, Huánuco, San Martín, Puno and Huancavelica were the poorest departments with a GDP per capita lower than USD PPP 6 000. In contrast, Moquegua was by far the richest department with a GDP per capita of over USD PPP 30 000, followed by Lima, Arequipa, Tacna and Ica with a GDP per capita above USD PPP 12 000 (Figure 1.6). Similarly, regional growth in the previous decade (2001-12) varied from 3.0% annually in Pasco to 8.5% in Ica (INEI, 2014).

Figure 1.6. GDP per capita per department, 2014

USD PPP 2014

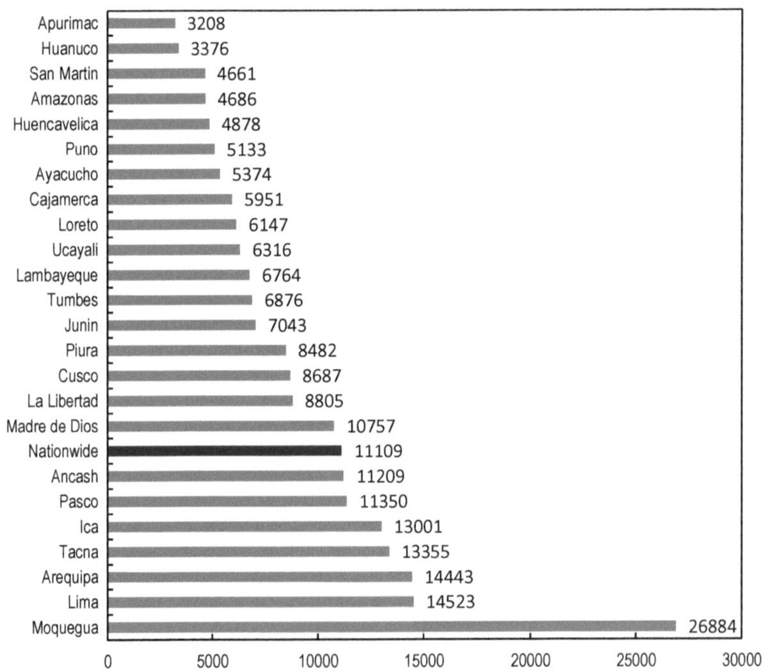

Source: INEI (2015), *Encuesta Nacional de Hogares, Instituto Nacional de Estadística e Informática.*

Peru ranked 84 out of 188 countries in the Human Development Index (HDI),[2] with a score of 0.734 in 2014, putting Peru in the high HDI-category (UNDP, 2015). In terms of standards of living, poverty and access to basic public services, there is however wide contrast between the coastal departments and the departments from the mountain ranges and rainforest. Lack of access to services is evidenced by the percentage of population with at least one basic need not met (Table 1.1), three times higher in rural populations in comparison to urban populations (INEI, 2014). Even more concerning is the fact that two thirds of the population in the rainforest region has at least one basic need unmet. Unsurprisingly, such marked regional disparities are reflected in the quality and availability of health services, which is further discussed in Chapter 2.

Table 1.1. Population with at least one basic need unmet

Percentage of total population

Scope	2007	2008	2009	2010	2011	2012 (est.)
Urban	19.1	19.5	18.5	15.8	15.8	14.4
Rural	59.1	53.5	49.6	46.5	44.9	43
Coast	16.4	17.5	16.5	14	14.5	12.9
Mountain ranges	41.9	36.5	32.5	28.8	27.4	26
Rainforest	57.3	56	55	52.5	49.6	46.9

Source: INEI (2014), *Encuesta Nacional de Hogares, Instituto Nacional de Estadística e Informática.*

High rates of informal labour are an embedded feature of Peruvian society

Unemployment rates in Peru were 4.2% of the available labour force in 2014 (World Bank, 2016). This rate was lower than both the average rate for Latin America and the Caribbean (6.3%) and that of the OECD countries (7.3%). However, like most emerging economies, Peru is characterised by a large shadow economy and a high incidence of informal employment. Several definitions of informality are in use, such as employees without a written contract, self-employed people without registered activity, or workers not contributing to pensions or health insurance.

The National Institute of Statistics and Informatics (*Instituto Nacional de Estadística e Informática*, INEI) use a broad definition of informal labour: any self-employed worker within the informal sector, salaried workers not contributing to pensions and unpaid family workers. Even though informal employment has decreased in Peru over the past years, under this definition, over 57% of Peruvian employment is in the informal sector, and over 74% of total employment is informal (Figure 1.7) – meaning, in effect, that almost half the employment in the formal sector could be defined as informal (INEI, 2014). When using ILO's definition of informal employment as a percentage of non-agricultural employment, Peru has one of the highest rates of Latin America at 70.6% (Figure 1.8).

Figure 1.7. Evolution of informal employment in Peru, 2007-12

As percentage of total employment

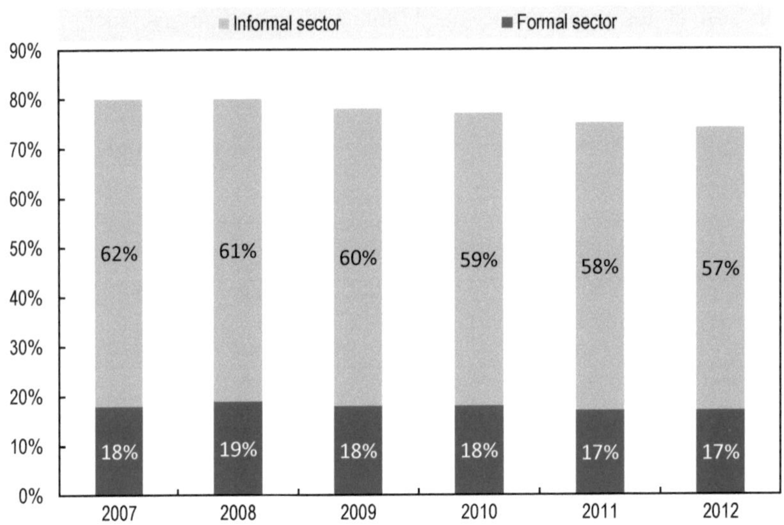

Source: INEI (2014), *Encuesta Nacional de Hogares, Instituto Nacional de Estadística e Informática.*

Figure 1.8. Informal employment in Latin America 2013 (or nearest year)

As percentage of non-agricultural employment

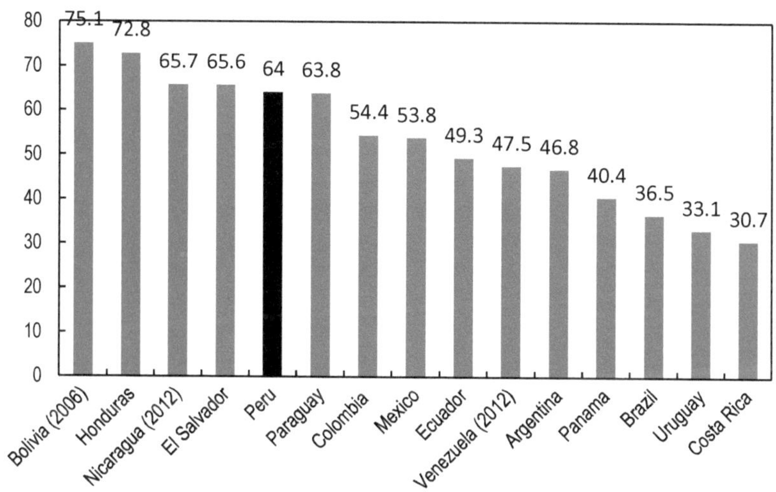

Source: ILO Department of Statistics, 2014.

The Peruvian economy tends to concentrate labour in less productive and typically informal activities such as agriculture. As a result, even though the informal sector employs roughly three out of every five Peruvians, it only accounts for a fifth of national GDP. The differences across departments in terms of informal employment explain disparities in economic growth outcomes: as explained earlier, some departments have a per capita GDP under USD PPP 6 000: Apurímac, Huánuco, San Martín, Amazonas, Huancavelica and Puno. As might be expected, these are the six departments with the highest informal labour rates. Similarly, the five richest departments report the lowest rates of informal labour (Figure 1.9).

Figure 1.9. Informal employment by department in 2013

Percentage of total employment

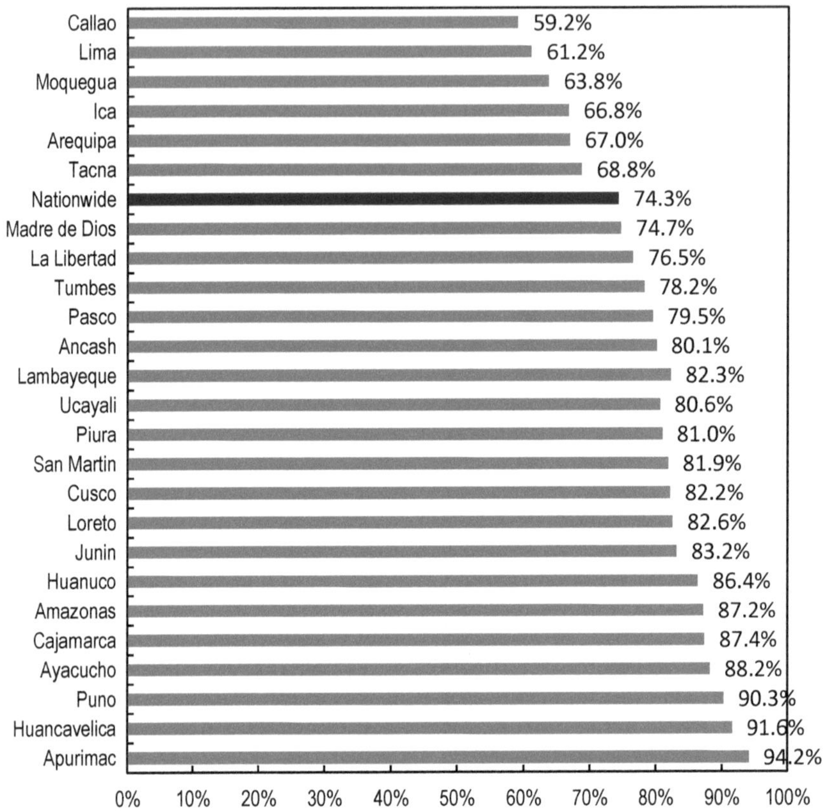

Source: INEI (2014), *Encuesta Nacional de Hogares, Instituto Nacional de Estadística e Informática.*

Nearly 17% of Peruvian urban youth are neither in employment nor in education or training (Málaga et al., 2014), compared to 12.6% on average across OECD countries (OECD, 2016). The situation is worse for young women, since approximately 26% of this group is neither in employment nor in education or training.

Peru's major health care needs stem from non-communicable diseases – but communicable disease and injuries remain a substantial burden

Although the Peruvian population is young, it nevertheless faces complex and challenging health care needs. These needs will inevitably develop in parallel with the demographic and epidemiologic transition that the country is undergoing. Of particular concern is Peru's increasing prevalence of chronic non-communicable disease, while the incidence of infectious diseases remains high.

Peru and other countries in Latin America are often described as having a "*triple burden of disease*". Chronic conditions, such as cardiovascular diseases, cancers or diabetes (also known as non-communicable diseases, NCDs), accounted for almost 50% of deaths in Peru in 2014 (Figure 1.10; MINSA, 2016). The main single cause of death in Peru in 2014 was cancer, accounting for 20% of all deaths, followed by cardiovascular diseases, which accounted for 19%. Nevertheless, communicable diseases remain important, accounting for 26% of deaths. Injuries accounted for 9%, indicating that they remain a substantial burden for the Peruvian population. Significant challenges around infectious disease control and maternal and child health thus persist in Peru; both under-five mortality and maternal mortality are close to the regional average (at 16.9 vs 17.9 deaths per 1 000 live births, and 68 vs. 67 per 100 000 live births respectively). Encouragingly, however, infant chronic malnutrition rates have been significantly reduced from 25.4% in 2000 to 14.4% in 2015. Nevertheless, in rural areas this rate remains very high at 24.6%, again exposing substantial geographic variation within the country. Moving from mortality to morbidity, IMHE data shows that the three main causes of disability in Peru are low back and neck pain, sensory disorders (such as loss of sight or hearing) and depressive disorders (http://www.healthdata.org/peru).

Figure 1.10. Causes of mortality in Peru in 2014

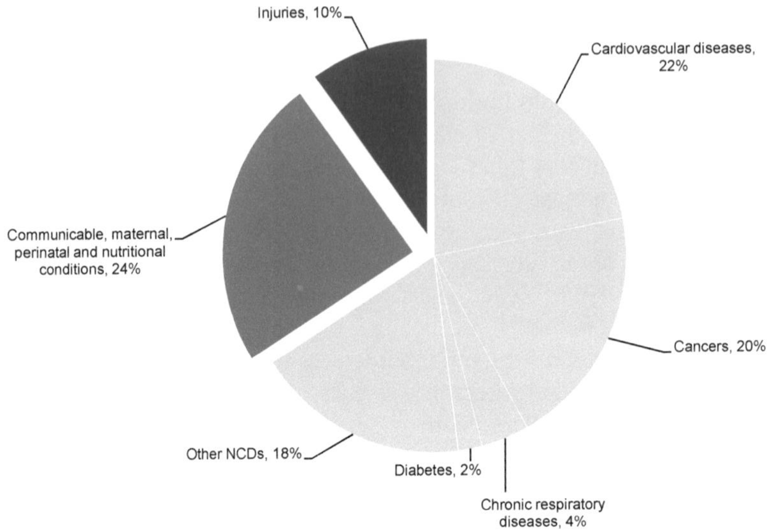

Source: MINSA (2016), "Instituciones Prestadoras de Servicios de Salud (IPRESS) en el marco del AUS", http://portales.susalud.gob.pe/web/cdi/ipress.

One of the most important health system interventions to control communicable disease concerns population vaccination programmes. After impressive increases in vaccination rates towards the end of the 20th century, vaccination rates in Peru stagnated or decreased from 2000 to 2015, as seen in Figure 1.11 (World Bank, 2016). While BCG vaccination remained relatively stable (93% of one year old children in 2000, as compared to 91% in 2015), measles vaccination coverage (in children aged 12-23 months) decreased from 97% in 2000 to 92% in 2015, and polio vaccination coverage (in one year-old children) fell from 93% to 87%. Similarly, DPT vaccination (in children aged 12-23 months) fell from 98% in 2000 to 90% in 2015. In addition, some region like Huancavelica reported DPT coverage of just 54.2% in 2012, demonstrating substantial geographical disparities in vaccination coverage (INEI, 2014).

Infectious diseases such as tuberculosis and malaria remain present in Peru, but have decreased in incidence over the last decade. In contrast, reported cases of dengue have increased exponentially in recent years. In 2006, 4 022 cases of dengue were recorded, but this number increased seven fold in six years to reach more than 28 000 cases in 2012 (INEI). This figure declined in 2013 but rose again to nearly 40 000 cases in 2015 (MINSA, 2016). Of similar concern, years of life lost due to HIV/AIDS increased by 357% from 1990 to 2010, as seen in Table 1.2.

Figure 1.11. Vaccination rates in Peru, 1985-2015

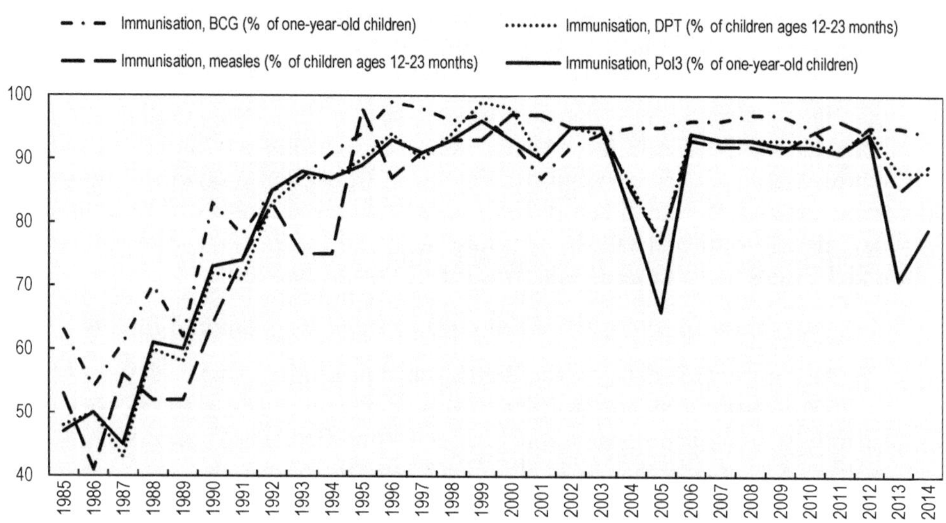

Source: World Bank (2016), "World Bank Open Data", http://data.worldbank.org/data-catalog/world-development-indicators/; MINSA (2016), "Instituciones Prestadoras de Servicios de Salud (IPRESS) en el marco del AUS", http://portales.susalud.gob.pe/web/cdi/ipress.

NCD's are closely associated with behavioural risk factors such as unhealthy diets and low physical activity leading to obesity, as well as smoking and harmful alcohol consumption. Hence, controlling these risk factors is a public health priority. In Peru, smoking prevalence is higher than the OECD average for men but lower for women: 34.6% of men and 8.3% of women over 15 years of age in Peru used tobacco daily in 2013, as compared to 24.2% and 15.5% respectively among OECD countries (OECD, 2016).

Alcohol consumption in Peru was on average 8.1 litres of pure alcohol per capita (in those aged over 15 years of age) between 2008 and 2010 (WHO, 2014). This was somewhat lower than the OECD average of 8.8 litres in 2013 (OECD, 2016). Nevertheless, 23.2% of the Peruvian population are affected by excessive alcohol consumption (35.2% of men and 12.7% of women).

Finally, obesity levels in Peru were higher than the average among OECD countries: 20.9% of the Peruvian adult population were obese in 2014 (15.5% among men and 18.3% among women), as compared to the OECD average of 19% in 2013. Given the high prevalence of risk factors in Peru, there is little reason to hope that the adverse trends on increased non-communicable diseases can be reversed in the middle term.

1.2. Towards universal health coverage in Peru

The share of the population formally enrolled in a health insurance scheme increased from 37% in 2004 to 83% in 2017, according to SUSALUD. This is important and welcome progress. Nevertheless, some one in seven Peruvians remain without health insurance. Furthermore, benefit packages across the different insurance schemes are not equal, and out-of-pocket (OOP) spending remains high. Substantial ground still needs to be covered, therefore, before UHC is fully achieved in Peru. This section describes in further detail the structure of the Peruvian health care system and the steps taken towards achieving UHC.

A universal entitlement to health care in Peru is enshrined by law

During the 1950s and 1960s, Peru's social protection policies developed in a fragmented fashion. In 1979, however, the universal right to social security was granted constitutional status for the first time. Social security underwent a major change in the 1990s, as the Private Pension System (*Sistema Privado de Pensiones*, SPP) was created. This introduced the *Individual Capitalisation Funding System* for the provision of old-age, disability, or death benefits. In health care, the General Health Law of 1997 divided the health care system into a universal public health sector and a private subsector. This law turned the state into a "subsidiary" agent rather than a "provider" agent and it promoted the participation of private firms under the supervision of the Superintendence of Health Care Providers (*Superintendencia de Entidades Prestadoras de Salud*, SEPS).

Another important milestone towards achieving universal health coverage (UHC) was the signing of the National Agreement (*Acuerdo Nacional*, AN) in 2002 by seven major political parties, seven civil society organisations and the government. The AN established four goals, underpinned by 31 policy guidelines to reach them. Health sector policies are included in the goal of "equity and social justice". Since the AN, the three governments that have succeeded have honoured the agreed policy guidelines. Even though they have shifted their emphasis over certain issues, successive governments have maintained the main goal set out in the AN of providing universal access to free, continuous, timely, quality health care to the priority population in poor areas and to the vulnerable population.

The goals within the AN have translated into a number of key policies, adopted over the following 14 years. First, the Integral Health Insurance (*Seguro Integral de Salud*, SIS) was created in 2001 to fund health services for Peruvians who, due to poverty, did not have health insurance. Second, in 2009, the Universal Health Insurance Law (*Aseguramiento Universal en Salud*, AUS) established the right to quality and timely health care services to all residents in Peru, aiming to improve financial protection for population groups without social security coverage. Third, the Peruvian Ministry of Health (*Ministerio de Salud del Perú*, MINSA) defined the Essential Health Insurance Plan (*Plan Esencial de Aseguramiento en Salud*, PEAS) in 2009. PEAS became the minimum benefits coverage for all Peruvians addressing 65% of the burden of disease, including explicit guarantees of timeliness and quality of service. Fourth, the financing sources and payment mechanisms for the subsidised and semi-contributory schemes were established in 2011 with the Law on Public Financing of Subsidised and Semi-Contributory Schemes. Another important step took place in 2013, when the National Health Superintendence (*Superintendencia Nacional de Salud*, or SUSALUD) was created with the mission to protect the health-related rights of Peruvians.

Box 1.1. Recent reforms to expand coverage of health insurance in Peru

- In 2001, the SIS was created aiming to covering all uninsured population (predominantly among low-income groups).
- In 2002, the AN was signed, aiming to universal access to health services to the poor and vulnerable population.
- In 2007, SIS created the semi-subsidised regime for people with low ability to pay.
- In 2008, access was given to microenterprises' workers in the semi-contributory regime with payments made by the employer and matched by the MEF.
- In 2009, the Universal Health Insurance Law (*Aseguramiento Universal de* Salud, AUS) included the semi-contributory regime.
- In 2013, a new attempt to include non-poor populations was made through SIS Entrepreneurs, which affiliated independent workers who signed up for the New Unique Simplified Regime (*Nuevo Régimen Único Simplificado*, NRUS) of the National Superintendence of Customs and Tax Administration (*Superintendencia Nacional de Aduanas y Administración Tributaria*, SUNAT). This tax regime was created as an incentive for independent workers to file taxes, and hence increase the tax base. Affiliation to SIS is automatic through this mechanism, since SUNAT provides the list to SIS of the population enrolled. No additional payments are required besides paying taxes.

More recently, in October 2015, a new AN agreement was signed that recognised the urgent need to close the gaps in access to health and to health social security, identifying four critical policy areas to improve access and health insurance coverage: health human resources; infrastructure and equipment; transfer of technologies, technological innovations, applied research in health and information systems; and financing. Reissuing the AN is a clear indication of the commitment of Peru to continue progress toward UHC.

Health care services in Peru are provided by a number of distinct insurer/provider institutes

The most distinctive feature of the Peruvian health system is its division into various subsystems. Each subsystem replicates the set of fundamental health system activities for its affiliated population, i.e. stewardship, revenue raising, purchasing services and providing those services (Figure 1.12). This means that functions which are increasingly organised horizontally (that is, in a unified nation-wide approach) in most OECD health systems, remain vertically organised for various and distinct population subgroups in Peru. To some extent, each health subsystem in Peru operates as a separate health system, within a much lighter-touch horizontal framework, and with little co-ordination of functions across them.

Figure 1.12. Structure of the Peruvian health system

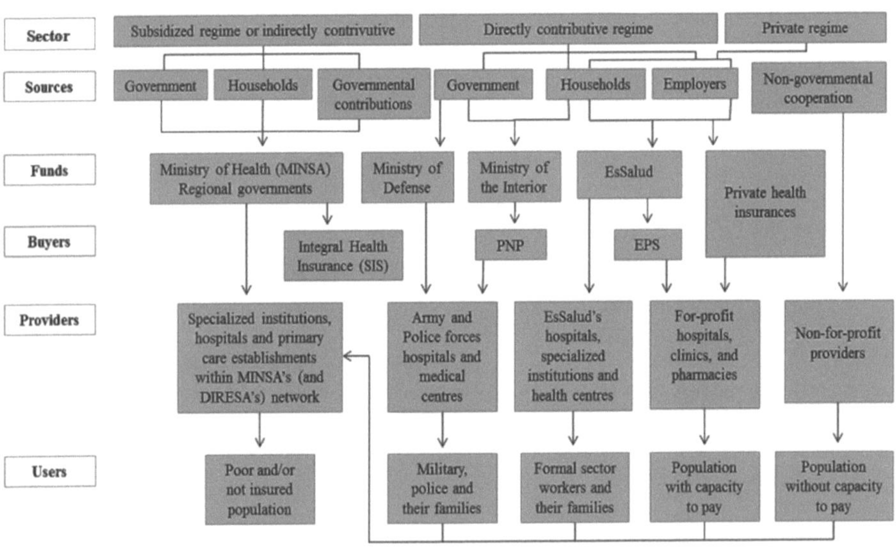

Source: Alcalde-Rabanal, J., O. Lazo-González and G. Nigeda (2011), "Sistema de salud de Perú", *Salud Pública de México*, Vol. 53:2.

All inhabitants in Peru are by law obliged to affiliate to the health care system; the specific scheme into which they enroll depends on their socio-economic characteristics. The *Seguro Social de Salud*, more commonly known as *EsSalud,* covers all salaried formal sector workers and their families. Separately, the Police and the Army are covered by the *Sanidad de la Policía Nacional* and the *Sanidad de las Fuerzas Armadas* respectively. Each of these three schemes owns and operates its own clinics and hospitals (Health Care Providers, *Instituciones Prestadoras de Servicios de Salud,* IPRESS). Benefits provided are in-kind (i.e. health care services), following broad provisions set in their corresponding legal frameworks, including preventive and curative services. Care should thus be provided at the IPRESS corresponding to the scheme-specific settings. In case of emergencies, patients can be treated in other institutions' facilities up to the point of medical stabilisation for later referral to the corresponding insured institution facilities.

As mentioned earlier, *Seguro Integral de Salud*, or SIS, was created in 2001 to fund health services for Peruvians who, due to poverty, did not have health insurance. SIS manages two regimes, first, the subsidised regime financed by general taxes and, second, the semi-contributory regime financed by household contributions and general taxes. The subsidised regime is targeted to the poor and vulnerable population. When SIS was created it covered only poor pregnant women, children under five and children in public schools. Later new groups were included until 2005 when the eligible population was defined as consisting of all the poor lacking health insurance. In 2013, coverage further expanded to cover the so-called vulnerable population (not necessarily only those being poor) which includes, among those not insured by other social security schemes, all children between 0-5 years of age, school age children, and pregnant women.

The "*insured population*" in Peru thus refers to the population who are covered either by a social security subsystem (*EsSalud,* the *Sanidad de la Policía Nacional* or the *Sanidad de las Fuerzas Armadas*), which provides health care, as well as pension and welfare coverage, or by SIS. There is also some coverage by private enterprises, although private health insurance covers only a small proportion of the Peruvian population.

Progress towards UHC has been achieved – although many Peruvians remain uninsured

In recent years, the main effort towards UHC in Peru has been to increase population health insurance coverage. Health insurance coverage in Peru has increased from 37% in 2004 to 83% in April 2017, indicating rapid and significant progress. SIS has been the key player in this effort. In 2015, SIS covered 43% of the population, while EsSalud covered 25% and the remaining types of insurances represented 5% of coverage (Figure 1.13). Overall, however, 17% of the Peruvian population still lacked health insurance in 2017.

Figure 1.13. Health insurance coverage in Peru, 2004-15

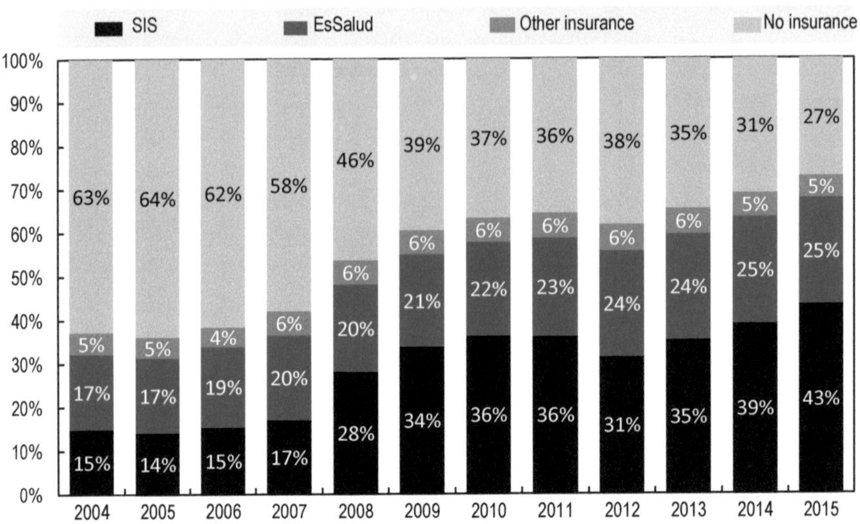

Source: INEI (2016), *Condiciones de Vida en el Perú*, Retrieved from Lima: https://www.inei.gob.pe/media/MenuRecursivo/boletines/informe-tecnico-n02_condiciones-vida_octnovdic15.pdf.

The Peruvian Government has undertaken substantial efforts to increase coverage across the whole country, targeting efforts especially to the most vulnerable groups. By 2011, SIS coverage in poor departments such as Huancavelica, Apurimac and Ayacucho reached levels above 80%. Mainly due to the implementation of SIS, 77.7% of the rural population now has some form of health insurance in 2014, as opposed to 66.3% of the urban population (see Figure 1.15). Importantly, 65% of SIS's beneficiaries were in the two lowest expenditure quintiles in 2004, rising up to 70.6% in 2012, a development that shows a pro-poor affiliation in SIS (see Figure 1.16). SIS was designed to primarily serve those in poverty and workers in small and medium-sized enterprises, and as such it has made a tremendous impact in reducing inequalities in access to health services.

Figure 1.15. Uninsured by geographical area, 2004-15

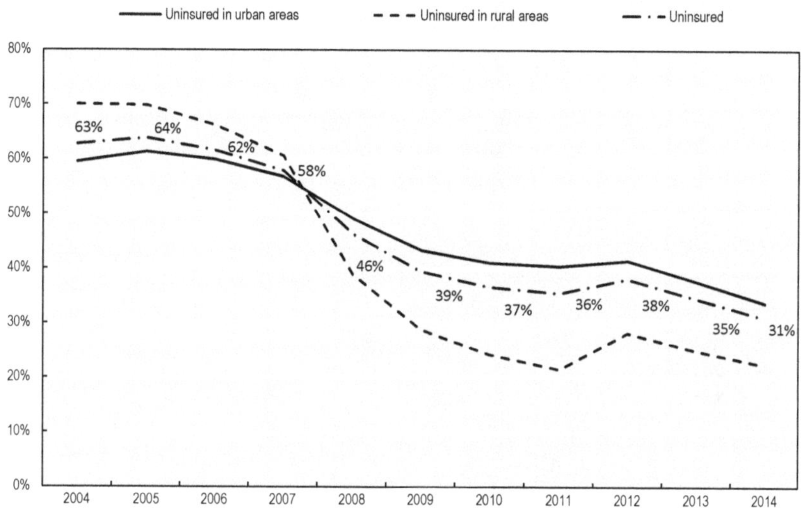

Source: INEI (2016), "Condiciones de Vida en el Perú", retrieved from: https://www.inei.gob.pe/media/MenuRecursivo/boletines/informe-tecnico-n02_condiciones-vida_octnovdic15.pdf.

Figure 1.16. SIS beneficiaries by expenditure quintiles, 2004-12

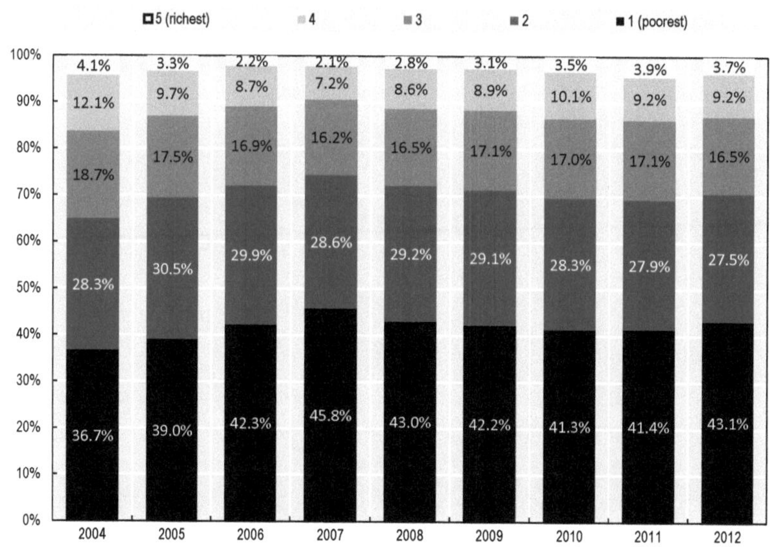

Source: MINSA (2015), "Cuentas nacionales de salud Perú 1995-2012", retrieved from http://bvs.minsa.gob.pe/local/MINSA/3248.pdf.

EsSalud's coverage has also increased, albeit at a slower rate, with annual expansion of averaging at 8.4% in recent years, well below that of SIS. EsSalud's coverage expansion is mainly due to economic growth in Peru and so is linked to urban areas and the working population. Overall, only 8.6% of the rural population is covered by EsSalud (compared to 90.8% covered by SIS), whilst EsSalud covers 57.6% of the total working population in urban areas (compared to 28.4% covered by SIS). Similarly, EsSalud covered 70.5% of formal workers in 2009 (compared to 35.9% covered by SIS). EsSalud also covered 9.3% of informal workers.

Nevertheless, despite the success of SIS in reaching groups not covered by EsSalud, lower-middle income groups – with an income between PEN 1 500 and 3 000 (USD 558 and USD 1 115) are reported as "falling between two stools" – they are not "poor enough" to benefit from insurance through SIS, but their employment as self-employed or informal workers means that they do not have coverage by EsSalud either. Given that at present, Peru does not have an affordable private health insurance market for these poorer groups, this group must either forego health care, or pay out-of-pocket.

Peru thus still lies behind most countries that have followed the path of health insurance to move towards UHC (Figure 1.17). Health insurance coverage has for example reached 95.7% in Colombia, 98.2% in Chile and 98.9% in Mexico. As health insurance coverage only reached 83% of Peruvians in 2017, much remains to be done to close this remaining gap.

Figure 1.17. Health insurance coverage in OECD countries (2013) and Peru (2014)

Percentage of the population

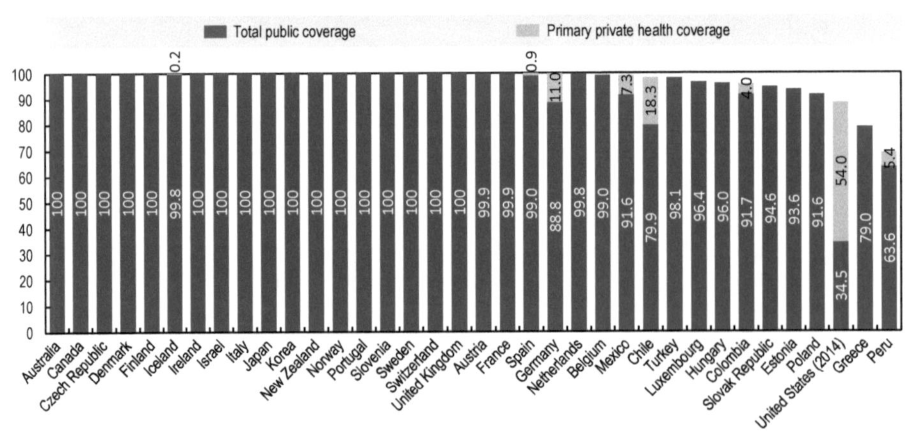

Source: *OECD Health Statistics 2016*, http://dx.doi.org/10.1787/health-data-en.

1.3. Key actors in Peru's health care system

Broadly, Peru's health system is both vertically integrated (with insurers and providers belonging to a single institution) and geographically decentralised. These insurer/provider networks, underpinned by strategic leadership from central and local government, have increased the coverage of effective health services in Peru. This section describes the roles and functions of major stakeholders within the Peruvian health care system which, in broad terms, is composed of the SIS, EsSalud and other subsystems.

Balancing centralised and decentralised responsibilities

Within the SIS subsystem, the Ministry of Health (MINSA) is the highest authority overseeing health care delivery. For SIS insurance and service delivery, MINSA is the ultimately accountable institute, directing and managing national health policy, as well as drafting and monitoring national health laws and regulations. At the same time, however, a drive toward regional decentralisation of executive power has been a major policy goal reform across several sectors in recent years. Greater cost-consciousness at the local level is expected to improve technical efficiency. In addition, local decision-makers' knowledge of local circumstances allows them to tailor services and spending patterns to local needs and preferences, which improves allocative efficiency.

An important step toward decentralisation of powers was taken in 2002 with the election of autonomous regional governments, with accompanying transfers of funds, regulatory powers and service obligations. The health public sector's decentralisation was completed between 2004 and 2009, in the fourth and final stage of the entire decentralisation process. Now, within SIS, regional governments manage all health services through Regional Health Directorates (*Direcciones Regionales de Salud*, DIRESA). The one exception concerns Lima. Until recently, the Institute for Management of Health Services was in charge of public hospitals in metropolitan Lima. This responsibility was transferred to MINSA in December 2016. This represents the only set of health services for which central government has direct responsibility.

The decentralisation process, however, did not always establish clear mechanisms to define priorities and policies that reflected the new relationship between the MINSA and the DIRESA. Currently, for example, the co-ordination between MINSA and DIRESA is limited to: i) the supply of inputs and medicines requested by DIRESA for their health strategies; and ii) SIS payments for health services provided to its beneficiaries. It has been reported that co-ordination and oversight of critical programmes, such as childhood vaccination, is not as strong as it could be. Although, DIRESA directors hold meetings with the Minister of Health to discuss health policy guidelines, the agreements are not legally binding (Francke, 2013), which risks weak commitment to work in line with the national guidelines.

Decentralisation has at times complicated the delivery of national programmes. It has been reported, for example, that the National Health Strategies which constitute MINSA's main operational activities (such as the national HIV/AIDS programme) have, at times, been weakened because of the decentralisation of funds, regulatory powers and service obligations. In broad terms, National Health Strategies remain in charge of centralised purchases of supplies and medicines, while the actual provision of care is managed regionally or locally. The effectiveness of regulation and supervision at local level has been questioned (Francke, 2013). Additionally, National Health Strategies are bound to the budgeting for results programmes under the guidance of the Ministry of Economics and Finance, which provides direct funding without participation or supervision of MINSA. As discussed in Chapter 3, this also risks weakening the latter's ability to supervise delivery of national strategies.

Multiple health insurers are responsible for managing clinical and financial risks in their affiliated populations

In addition to the arrangements pertaining to SIS described above, several other institutions offer health care insurance and health care services in Peru. As mentioned earlier, the major institutes offering contributory health insurance/services are EsSalud and the Army and Police forces schemes, as well as private sector insurance companies and private health providers (*Entidades Prestadoras de Salud*, EPS). The contributory health insurance institutions, along with the subsidised health insurance institution (SIS), collectively form the Institutions for the Administration of Health Insurance Funds (*Instituciones Administradoras de Fondos de Aseguramiento en Salud*, IAFAS).

Peru's Universal Health Insurance Law (*Aseguramiento Universal en Salud*) mandates that all schemes within IAFAS are obliged to offer a mimimum package of care, which is called the Essential Health Insurance Plan (*Plan Esencial de Aseguramiento en Salud*) or PEAS. This basic package was established in 2009, through a burden of disease study, with complementary budget-impact and cost-effective analyses. In order to ensure adequate funding and provision of the PEAS, the National Superintendence for Health Insurance (*Superintendencia Nacional de Aseguramiento en Salud*, SUNASA) was established. At the end of 2013, SUNASA changed its name to SUSALUD (*Superintendencia Nacional de Salud*).

Box 1.2. Institutions providing health care insurance and health care services in Peru

Public health insurance schemes

- *EsSalud*: contributory health insurance compulsory for wage earners, offering medical care in case of illness, accidents and maternity, as well as subsidised pharmaceuticals. Families of EsSalud's beneficiaries are also covered, as well as members of co-operatives from both the private and public sector and independent workers that choose to affiliate.
- *Army health insurance*: contributory health insurance for population groups working for the armed forces, offering medical attention for illness, accidents and maternity.
- *Police health insurance*: contributory health insurance for populations groups working for the police forces, offering medical attention for illness, accidents and maternity.
- *SIS*: a non-contributory health insurance that offers basic medical services. It was created in 2001 by combining the free school insurance (*Seguro Escolar Gratuaito)* and the maternal and child insurance (*Seguro Materno Infantil*) and aimed at covering all uninsured population. In 2005, the coverage of SIS was extended to young adults over 17, and in January 2015 to all age groups.

Private health insurance schemes

- *Private insurance companies*: offers complementary health benefits to individuals that choose to affiliate.
- *EPS*: health insurance provided by the health provision entities. Since 1978, public health insurance funds are allowed to transfer the provision of some health services to the EPS. From 1997, EPS are also allowed to offer complementary health benefits.

The Universal Health Insurance Law also mandates that the PEAS should be gradually expanded to cover more services. Currently, there are differences in the level of coverage offered by SIS (that is, PEAS) compared to that offered by EsSalud and the Army and Police Forces. In theory, these contributory schemes cover for health care needs, not just those in PEAS. At the same time, however, even affiliates of EsSalud sometimes seek private health care services or SIS services due to long waiting times. This phenomenon is explored further in Section 2.1.

Health care services are provided through Institutions of Health Services Provision (IPRESS) networked to specific insurers

The Institutions of Health Services Provision (*Instituciones Prestadoras de Servicios de Salud,* IPRESS) are responsible for actually delivering health services. There are public, private and mixed IPRESS – and they are under the supervision of the National Health Superintendence (*Superintendencia Nacional de Salud*, SUSALUD). Health services for SIS affiliates are provided by a network of establishments of the MINSA (including specialised hospitals and institutions). EsSalud provides health services to their affiliated population through their own facilities; similarly, the population affiliated to the Army and the Police forces health insurance receives health services from another specific network of health care providers. Each health insurance scheme in Peru thus offers health care services through its own network of providers.

In 2014, 8 895 IPRESS were registered, almost half being primary health care centres (MINSA, 2016). Around 600 IPRESS (7%) belonged to the private sector, out of which 37% were hospitals and 63% were primary health care centres. By the end of 2016, more than 20 000 health care centres, both public and private, were registered at RENIPRESS, the National Registry of Institutions of Health Services Provision, managed by SUSALUD. Searching the registry is public and is available through the website of SUSALUD. SUSALUD is also the institution responsible for the Register of Affiliates to health insurance schemes, to promote people's awareness of their entitlements. The Affiliates Register is publicly available online for anyone with a Peruvian ID number (DNI), including via smartphone Apps.

In some rural and isolated areas of Peru, it is still difficult to access primary health care services. 14% of people not attending health care services in 2010 mentioned distance as a barrier, particularly in Peru's Amazonas and mountainous regions. In order to tackle this, a National Health Plan for Indigenous People has been established. As well as developing access to modern facilities, the plan also recognises traditional medicine as a valued component of the health system. Traditional practitioners (such as shamans) are therefore considered as additional, informal, health providers within Peru's health care system.

Importantly, the government has started to promote exchange between provider networks, which is a step towards better integration within the health care system. This initiative is still limited to normative and operational restrictions (Seinfeld and Besich, 2014). Moreover, only 30% of patients affiliated to SIS in need of health care services were attended in a MINSA or regional government establishment, evidencing a lack of effective health care access. Regardless of affiliation, however, any patient can seek health care services at public facilities. At these facilities, SIS members have free services, while members of other affiliation schemes have to pay a subsidised fee (and uninsured individuals pay out-of-pocket).

Human resources for health, as well as hospital beds are scarce and unevenly distributed

Peru depends on 1.71 practicing doctors and 2.16 practicing nurses per 1 000 population (INEI, 2014), markedly less than the OECD averages of 3.3 and 9.1 respectively (Figures 1.18 and 1.19). The WHO estimated that countries with fewer than 2.5 physicians, nurses and midwives per 1 000 population generally fail to achieve adequate coverage rates for key health care interventions (WHO, 2006). Encouragingly, expansion of the health care workforce has been achieved during recent years (in 2002, physician and nurse density was only 1.4 and 0.8 respectively).

Figure 1.18. Practicing doctors per 1 000 population, 2000 and 2015 (or nearest year)

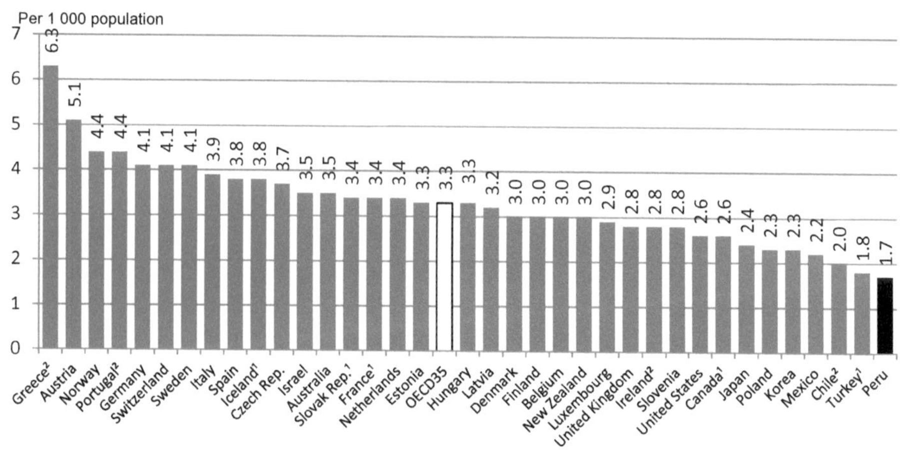

1. Data include not only doctors providing direct care to patients, but also those working in the health sector as managers, educators, researchers, etc. (adding another 5-10% of doctors).

2. Data refer to all doctors licensed to practice (resulting in a large over-estimation of the number of practising doctors in Portugal, of around 30%).

Source: *OECD Health Statistics 2016*, http://dx.doi.org/10.1787/health-data-en.

Figure 1.19. Practicing nurses per 1 000 population, 2015 (or nearest year)

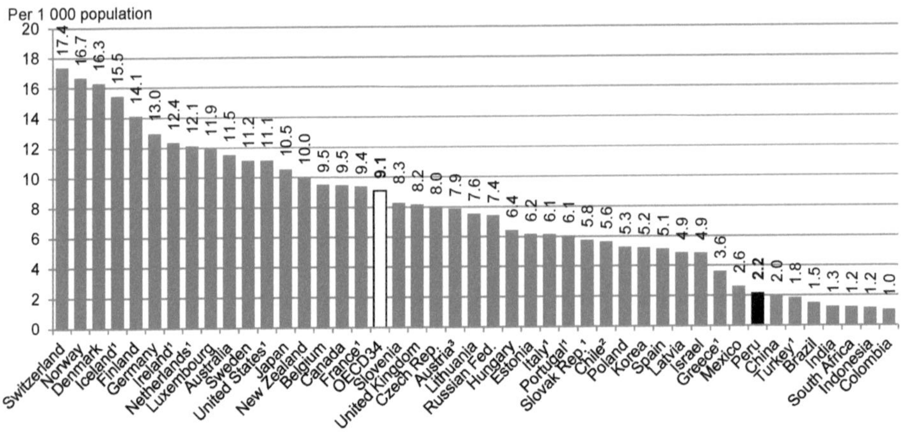

1. Data include not only nurses providing direct care to patients, but also those working in the health sector as managers, educators, researchers, etc.

2. Data in Chile refer to all nurses who are licensed to practice (less than one-third are professional nurses with a university degree).

3. Austria reports only nurses employed in hospital.

Source: *OECD Health Statistics 2016*, http://dx.doi.org/10.1787/health-data-en.

Health care workers are not evenly distributed within the country – but centralised mostly to the capital and the coastal regions. In 2009, Lima had for example a physician density over five times higher than Cajamarca (15.4 and 2.83 physicians per 10 000 inhabitants respectively) (MINSA, 2011). Moreover, Lima concentrated 53% of physicians, 40% of nurses and 44% of dentists (Alcalde-Rabanal, 2011).

Peru has seen an increase in medical faculties from 13 in 1960 to 28 in 2002 (Alcalde-Rabanal, 2011). Medical graduates have also increased from 951 in 1993 to 1 238 in 2003, an annual medical growth rate of 4% (comfortably exceeding the population growth rate of 1.8% during the same time period). Nevertheless, a shortage of human health capital in Peru remains. As discussed further in Chapter 2, continued expansion of the health care workforce will be vital to improve health care access and quality in the future.

Peru reports a density of 1.5 hospital beds per 1 000 population, which is lower than the average of 4.8 beds per 1 000 population among OECD countries (see Figure 1.20). It is also lower than the hospital bed density in Chile and Mexico (2.2 and 1.6 beds per 1 000 population respectively), which report the lowest density among OECD countries (OECD, 2016). 50% of hospital beds in use within the Peruvian health care system in 2005 belonged to MINSA's hospitals, while 20.7% and 21.6% belonged to the armed forces and to the private sector respectively (Alcalde-Rabanal, 2011).

Figure 1.20. Hospital beds in OECD and selected countries, 2000 and 2015

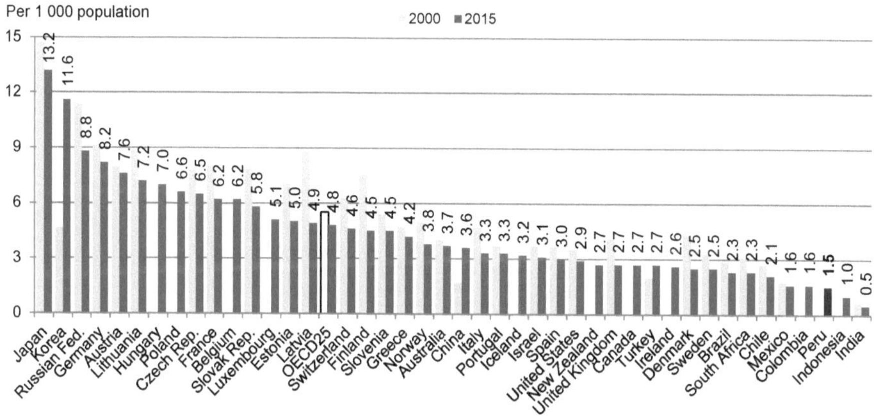

Source: *OECD Health Statistics 2016*, http://dx.doi.org/10.1787/health-data-en.

1.4. Systems to raise and distribute health care resources

Health care expenditure in Peru is relatively low, meaning that the health care system appears underfunded by international standards. Resources are also fragmented over the different subsystems, creating inequalities for access. OOP levels in Peru are also high, creating barriers of access, as well as the risk of catastrophic health spending in poorer families. Peru, has, however, been very innovative in the payment systems it uses, aiming to consolidate financial sustainability and improve the performance of the health care system. This chapter describes how the health care system is financed, and revenues are raised and distributed.

The health care system in Peru is underfunded by international standards

Health care in Peru is less well-resourced than all OECD health systems. Peru spent 5.4% of GDP on health in 2015, substantially less than the OECD average of 8.9% (Figure 1.21; World Bank, 2016; and OECD, 2016). Peru's spending equates to USD PPP 656 per capita per year, 5.5 times less than the OECD average of USD PPP 866 in 2015 (Figure 1.22), although differences in local prices mean that the real impact of this differential in per capita spending is likely to be substantially less.

The share of health system expenditure coming from public sources was 58.7% in Peru. This is also is a low level as compared to the OECD average of 73%, implying that private, non-pooled resources still constitute a large source of health system funding in Peru. Public expenditure in health is approximately USD 358 per capita, which is almost eight times less than the OECD average of USD 2 854 per capita (although, again, differences in local prices mean that a direct comparison of per capita absolute spending can be misleading).

Figure 1.21. Health expenditure as a share of GDP, 2015 (or nearest year)

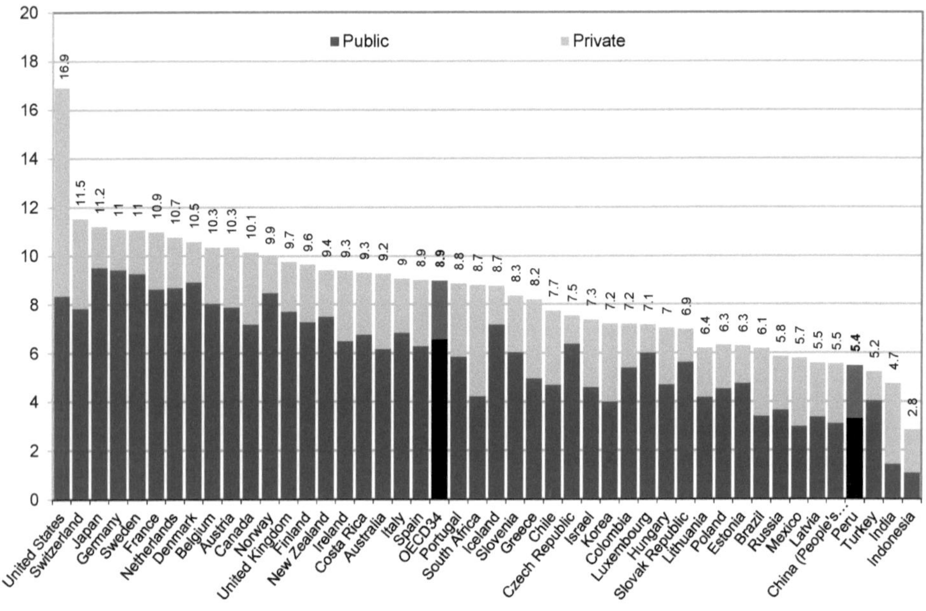

Note: Excluding investments unless otherwise stated.

Source: OECD Health Statistics 2016; WHO Global Health Expenditure Database; World Bank (2016), "World Development Indicators", retrieved from: http://databank.worldbank.org/data/reports.aspx?source=world-development-indicators.

Figure 1.22. Health expenditure per capita in USD PPP, 2015 (or nearest year)

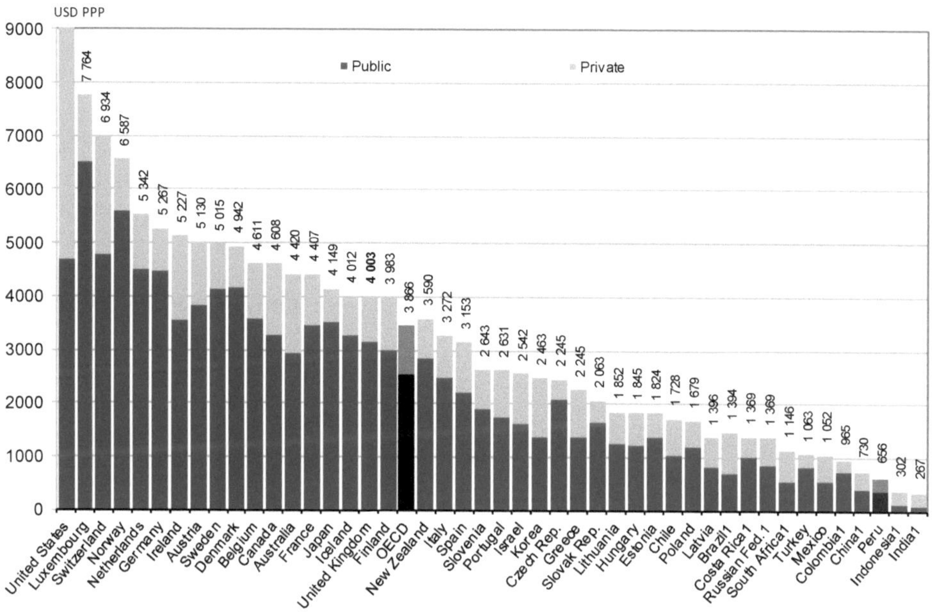

Note: Expenditure excludes investments, unless otherwise stated.

1. Includes investments.

2. Data refers to 2012.

Source: *OECD Health Statistics 2016*; WHO Global Health Expenditure Database; World Bank (2016), "World Development Indicators", retrieved from: http://databank.worldbank.org/data/reports.aspx?source=world-development-indicators.

Turning specifically to the SIS subsystem, expansion of affiliation has not always been accompanied by the necessary increase in financial resources. SIS recently undertook an actuarial study, using 2012 data. This study established an average expected cost of PEN 360 (around USD 110) per affiliate per year. In 2014, SIS's average expenditure per affiliate was only PEN 71 (around USD 22), which represents a mere 20% of the expected cost. It is unlikely that much of this low expenditure can be explained by technical efficiency. It is much more likely that this low expenditure represents real under-resourcing. Effective health insurance coverage may not be sustainable in the long run without adequate financing. Strains are already evident given that, as discussed in Section 2.1, SIS affiliates are increasingly by-passing SIS services and opting for private providers or self-medication from pharmacies.

Out-of-pocket spending for health services is relatively high

Out-of-pocket (OOP) spending in Peru constituted 29% of health system revenue in 2015; much higher than the OECD average of 19% and only below Korea (36.9%) and Mexico (44.7%), when compared to OECD countries. When compared to other Latin American countries, however, Peru's OOP expenditure on health is below the regional average of 34% (Figure 1.23). With OOP levels reaching 29% of total health care expenditure in Peru, they make up a substantial source of health system revenues.

Figure 1.23. Out-of-pocket expenditure in Peru and other Latin American countries, 2015

Percentage total expenditure on health

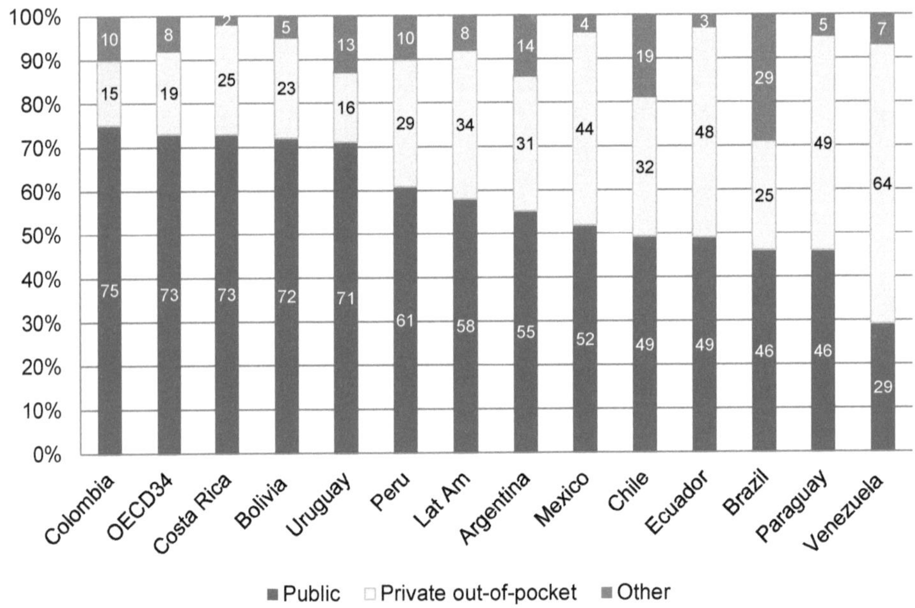

Source: WHO Global Health Expenditure Database.

High OOP spending may lead to people not accessing health care services or, alternatively, risking catastrophic health expenditure (CHE).[3] Ten per cent of people not accessing health care services in 2013, despite a need to do so, mentioned a lack of money as a barrier of access (ECLAC, 2013; and Congreso de la República, 2014). This indicator has however greatly improved after the implementation of new payment systems for purchasing health care services (see later in this section).

Uninsured population groups that decide to seek health care services nevertheless risks big economic burden. Indeed, 5% of Peruvian households experienced catastrophic health expenditure, adjusted for household composition, in 2012 (Seinfeld and Besich, 2014). This percentage was higher than the CHE levels in comparable countries such as Costa Rica, Colombia and Mexico (0.7%, 2.7% and 4.3% respectively), although lower than the CHE levels in Chile (11.1%).

Revenues within the Peruvian health care system are raised from multiple public and private sources

Three modes of health insurance financing are established within the Peruvian health care system i) the contributory regimes, principally EsSalud and the Armed Forces and Police health insurance schemes (financed by affiliates' or employers' contributions); ii) the semi-contributory regime (partially publicly financed), and iii) the subsidised regime (completely publicly financed). The majority of SIS affiliates are in the subsidised regime offered to the most vulnerable population. The semi-contributory regime make up a minority of SIS affiliates, covering i) independent workers who are not poor but nor have money enough to enrol into a private insurance, and ii) employees from small companies that do not have EsSalud coverage (Seinfeld and Besich, 2014).

Public funds come from the national budget credits that are assigned for health care on an annual basis, as well as from the contributions of the population affiliated to the contributory and the semi-contributory regime, regional and local governments and other co-operative revenues. The current legal framework however states that the contributions to the Social Health Insurance should only be used to provide health services to EsSalud's beneficiaries and can therefore not be pooled to create one unique health fund benefitting the population as a whole. The different subsystems within the Peruvian health care system are therefore financed with revenues that are tailored to the specific regimes; SIS, EsSalud and the Army and Police health insurances pool their funds separately, meaning that each institution has its own financial risk pool (Class et al., 2014).

Turning specifically to the SIS subsystem, 94% of total budget is resourced from general taxes, while the remaining 6% comes from donations and contributions by regional governments, international co-operation organisms, public and private institutions and transactions from an intangible health solidarity fund (Fondo Intangible Solidario de Salud; Alcalde-Rabanal, 2011).

EsSalud, on the other hand is financed mainly by a 9% payroll tax contribution made by employers and a 4% contribution from the revenues of retired population. Given Peru's high number of informal workers, the contributions to EsSalud are not as extensive as they could be. In addition, two reforms have reduced EsSalud' funding – and created significant challenges for the financial sustainability of this institution.

First, the Law of Modernisation of Health Social Security introduced private health insurance companies and providers (Figure 1.24), aiming to shift part of the demand for health care within EsSalud to the private sector. EsSalud beneficiaries can now choose to affiliate to a private insurer (EPS) that provide coverage for more frequent and low-cost services (denominated as the "*simple layer*") and other additional packages. Services not covered by the EPS are still covered by EsSalud. This simple layer coverage is financed by part of the employers' contribution to the Social Health Insurance: 2.25% (or 25% of the contribution) shifted to EPS and the remaining 6.75% (or 75% of the contribution) remains in EsSalud. The motivation behind this reform was to shift provision of more frequent, low-cost services to the private sector. For this system to work, the funds directed to EsSalud must cover the expected cost of the higher-cost services that it still covers. There are however no available studies to determine these costs. According to MINSA, in January 2015 EsSalud covered 7.8 million people, while EPS covered 743 000, or about 10% of all of EsSalud coverage. An additional point to note is that families with EPS coverage tend to be higher income families within EsSalud.

Figure 1.24. Health social security system

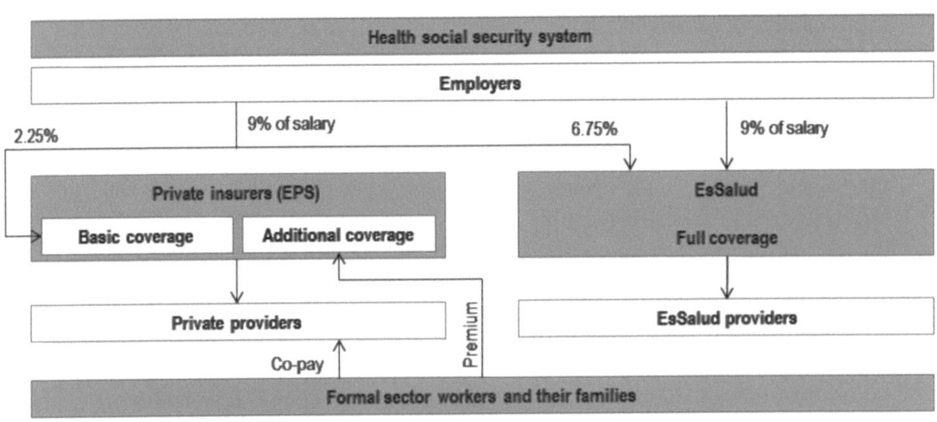

Second, EsSalud's income was temporarily reduced as part of the anti-crisis plan in 2009. It used to collect 9% of wages from employers over

15 salaries each year (one per month, plus additional salaries in July for Independence Day, in December for Christmas, and an additional salary allocated to unemployment insurance). The 2009 anti-crisis plan reallocated the extra 9% collected in July and December to the worker as an incentive to increase consumer spending in the wider economy. In 2015, this transitional change was made permanent, reducing EsSalud's resourcing in the long run.

An analysis of the implications of these reductions in contributory income is included in the 2012 actuarial study for EsSalud. According to this study, contributions received were 8.43% of salaries, below the expected 9%. This is due to the deviation of funds towards private EPS, as described earlier. Going forward, the salary contribution needed to achieve financial equilibrium was estimated to be between 9.7% and 10.38%. These figures suggest that EsSalud may face serious financial problems in the future, unless salary contributions are increased.

New payment systems could consolidate the financial sustainability and improve the performance of the Peruvian health care system

EsSalud and the Army and Police health scheme both provide insurance to their affiliated population, as well as purchase health care services from their own networks of providers. SIS, on the other hand, purchases health services from MINSA's facilities or from regional governments. In the past there were multiple different regional payment systems within MINSA but since, a single national policy was introduced; basic payment and four additional components: i) performance payments; ii) regional bonus; iii) bonus for primary care providers or for hospital specialists; iv) bonus for additional responsibilities.

Another major initiative to improve both the health of the Peruvian population, as well as the financial sustainability of the Peruvian health care system, was the introduction of results based financing (*Presupuesto por Resultado*, PpR) for MINSA services in 2007. By 2015, 81 different budget programmes, giving priority to vulnerable populations such as children, pregnant women and poor population, had been established. This payment system includes monitoring and benchmarking performance of health care services and health indicators in order to drive health care quality improvements. Impressive improvements have been achieved with these payment systems. Between 2000 and 2007, the expenditure on individual health increased by an annual average of 5% – but chronic malnutrition among children was held constant (Congreso de la República, 2014). With the introduction of PpR, the expenditure associated to child health increased with 140% from 2008 to 2014, from PEN 1 312 million (around

USD 404 000) to PEN 2 457 million (around USD 757 000) and chronic malnutrition among children was halved from 28% in 2008 to 14% in 2016.

Likewise, the percentage of infants below 1 year of age vaccinated against pneumococci and rotavirus increased from 25% in 2009 to 75.6% in 2014, with similar increases both in urban and rural settings. Achievements in terms of access to care for non-communicable diseases have also been made. The economic barrier, impeding people in need from seeking health care services has also been reduced from 25% in 2004 to 10% in 2013. Inevitably, PpR schemes add complexity to accountability mechanisms and resource flows, much of which is handled by the Ministry of Economy and Finances (MEF). This implies a reduced stewardship role for MINSA, as discussed further in Chapter 3, Section 3.2.

1.5. Information systems underpinning health care delivery

Health information systems have a vital role to underpin operational and strategic decision-making. Information systems in Peru, however, are fragmented between the different insurer/provider institutes, making it difficult to undertake comprehensive analysis of system performance, or provide comparisons of performance across providers. Innovations on information systems are nonetheless on the way in Peru. This section describes the health information systems used in Peru in further detail.

Information systems are generated by several key actors

The National Statistics and Informatics Institute (*Instituto Nacional de Estadística e Informática*, INEI) is a crucial institution for information systems, since it is responsible for producing statistical information about demographic development, vital statistics, the demographic and family health questionnaire and the continuous household questionnaire among other resources. In addition, the public health information network is in charge of MINSA, which manages the production, analysis, publication and use of information on public health surveillance. Another key institution at national level is the National Health Institute (*Instituto Nacional de Salud*, INS). The INS promotes, develops and diffuses scientific research.

Peru's information infrastructure, particularly quality information, includes a range of core health system data. The Health Information System (HIS) is a software tool that records outpatient activities, and can be processed and consulted by health personnel. The HIS is the source of basic information of daily outpatient care recording attendance to health facilities, epidemiological surveillance in terms of morbidity, and preventive and promotional activities. Vaccination services, antenatal and child health checks are reported. So too are hospital indicators, including admissions, bed numbers, reasons for admission, and certain activities. HIS should be reported on a monthly basis by MINSA health establishments, but, due to the fragmented information systems, it is not reported by EsSalud or other subsystems, limiting the use of the information. However, SUSALUD manages wide range of information (for example: health resources, ambulatory care, emergencies, hospitalisation, births, institutional surveillance events, surgeries) from public and private institutions through SETI-IPRESS.

Like many other domains of the Peruvian health system, however, the information system is fragmented between subsystems. Both EsSalud and the private stakeholders generate their own, separate information system. This fragmentation makes it difficult to compare different population segments and get a comprehensive picture about health care performance.

Modern information systems in Peru are developing

In recent years, mayor achievements in information technologies and communications have been accomplished in Peru. In 2011, an agenda for digital information in Peru was updated, establishing an online government to allow citizens to access information related to different public services. In the health care sector, the General Office of Statistics and Informatics (*Oficina General de Estadística e Informática*, OGEI) of the MINSA, has developed norms and directives for information systems, creating a conceptual framework in accordance to international guidelines developed by the WHO and the International Organization for Standardization (Curioso, 2014). The OGEI has implemented several digital systems benefitting the Peruvian population (see Box 1.4).

Box 1.4. Digital health information technologies developed in Peru

- Online registration of birth – directly after delivery, the health professional attending a new birth will go online to enter the id of the mother, basic birth information such as the newborn's weight, as well as its fingerprint. By immediate registration, the id of the newborn will be generated faster, thus allowing for immediate affiliation into SIS and other benefit programmes (Curioso et al., 2013b).
- *GeoMinsa* – is a platform based on Google Maps in order to show users the location, as well as the services offered by all health care providers in Peru. It also allows the user to find all the contact details, as well as fastest way to access the facilities.
- *Cuida tu Salud Móvil* – is a campaign consisting of sending text messages to registered users in order to promote healthy lifestyles. The text messages contain recommendations to prevent cancer, information about the importance of physical activity, nutrition, and the dangers of tobacco, alcohol and other substances.
- TeleHealth – by using information and communication technologies to build up a telehealth system, health professional can gain a greater accessibility to offer consultation, education and disease diagnosis of patients in rural and isolated areas. This way, a solution to health needs of vulnerable population groups can be achieved through remote health services, thus surpassing the limits of geographical barriers.
- Online medical appointment – is a service offered to patients who already have a medical record within MINSA's health establishments and who needs another appointment. Patients can then schedule a new appointment easier, avoiding long waiting times at the facilities.

Source: Curioso, W.H. (2014), "eSalud en Perú: Implementación de políticas para el fortalecimiento de sistemas de información en salud", *Panamerican Journal of Public Health,* Vol. 35(5/6), pp. 437-441, retrieved from http://bit.ly/1r5lAU5.

Information on quality of care is limited, and captures only part of the health system and population

To date, the focus of Peru's information infrastructure has been focused on activities, child and maternal health, and infectious diseases. This has been appropriate, given Peru's disease profile, but now needs expanding to cover more non-communicable diseases, in line with the changing epidemiological burden. Additionally, not enough is known about performance – data on patient outcomes is not available, nor is information on costs. However, SUSALUD tracks information about billing, according to RS 094-2013-SUNASA/CD and RS 020-2016-SUSALUD/S.

Some information on quality of care is available, but at this stage Peru would only be able to report a small number of 50 plus OECD Health Care Quality Indicators (HCQI). The OECD's review 2017 of Peru's health data system, *Monitoring Health System Performance in Peru: Data and Statistics*, includes a fuller discussion of health care quality information, in which some particular weaknesses are identified.

In particular, the fragmentation of the health system leads to incomplete data reporting. In most cases administrative data used to construct quality of care indicators is only collected from public institutions reporting to the HIS-MINSA system. In some cases, the construction of indicators based on this incomplete data leads to significant underestimations or inaccuracies. For instance, for hospital admission rates the denominator represents the whole population, while the numerator is based on public hospital facilities with only partial reporting by private facilities. Being able to collect data from all hospitals in Peru, regardless of ownership and affiliation, would increase international comparability. It would also make hospital-based indicators more useful indicator for comparing different segments of the population to inform domestic policy, since different population groups in practice use separate health systems. At present Peru's data is essentially based on the subset of the population using public hospitals and facilities, which means that this population subset is also not a representative sample for the whole population.

Coding practices around principal and secondary diagnoses, and also problems with linking data are also issues that affect Peru's capacity to gather and report information on health care quality. For instance, Peru is currently unable to link prescription data to individual diagnoses, and unable to link diagnosis data to death registries and therefore cannot calculate relative survival rates in cancer. In terms of prescribing practices, the difficulty in Peru is again around how to attribute the consumption to the right population denominator. In principle it is the SIS insured population, but it is unclear if this is strictly followed in the data collection. For example, it probably also includes antibiotics prescribed to other patients visiting public facilities.

Although the survey instruments which Peru has developed provide a substantial amount of valuable information, the various dimensions of medical quality outlined require investment in administrative data systems. The current survey tools do provide essential information and are likely to be important for future health systems development, but they need to be complemented with a system of administrative records with national coverage both in terms of geography and insurance affiliation. The implementation of a unique patient identifier, facilitating greater linkages of information for instance through common definitions and technologies, and further progress on coding practices are all needed in Peru, as OECD's review explores in greater detail (see OECD, 2017).

Conclusions

Although the Peruvian population is young, it faces complex and challenging health care needs, which will be accentuated by the country's rapid demographic and epidemiologic transition. Particularly worrying are Peru's increasing rates of non-communicable diseases, while infectious diseases remain an important burden. Given the high prevalence of adverse risk factors, there is little reason to hope that the adverse trends on chronic conditions will be reversed in the coming years. The Peruvian health care system therefore needs to control prevalent infectious diseases, as well as promote healthy lifestyles.

Important progress toward UHC within the Peruvian health care system has been achieved. Insurance coverage has increased from 37% in 2004 to 83% in 2017, according to the latest estimates from SUSALUD. The Peruvian health care system remains, however, fragmented into several subsystems, with little integration among them. Disparities between different affiliation schemes exist, leading to socio-economic and geographic inequalities in access and quality. Moreover, the health care system in Peru appears to be underfinanced, leading to restricted access to services. A considerable increase in national health care spending and a decrease in OOP expenditure are fundamental for further progress towards effective and equitable UHC.

Notes

1. The Gini coefficient measures the inequality across levels of income. A Gini coefficient of zero expresses perfect equality (where everyone has the same income). A Gini coefficient of one (or 100%) expresses maximal inequality (where only one person has all the income and all others have none).
2. The Human Development Index is a summary measure that combines indices of health, education and living standards.
3. Households using more than 40% of non-food expenditures to pay for health care are classed as experiencing Catastrophic Health Expenditure (CHE).

References

Alcalde-Rabanal, J., O. Lazo-González and G. Nigeda (2011), "Sistema de salud de Perú", *Salud Pública de México*, Vol. 53:2.

Class, D. et al. (2014), *Peru – Health Financing Profile*, World Bank Group, Washington, DC.

Congreso de la República (2014), "Sustentación del presupuesto del sector salud para el año 2015 en el congreso de la república por parte del ministro de salud", Aníbal Velásquez Valdivia, http://www.minsa.gob.pe/portalweb/lineamientos/archivos/141127_Discurso_SMS_Sustentacion_al_Congreso_de_Presupuesto_2015.pdf.

Curioso, W.H. (2014), "eSalud en Perú: Implementación de políticas para el fortalecimiento de sistemas de información en salud", *Panamerican Journal of Public Health*, Vol. 35(5/6), pp. 437-441, http://bit.ly/1r5lAU5.

Curioso, W.H., K. Pardo and M. Loayza (2013a), "Transformando el sistema de información de nacimientos en el Perú", *Rev Peru Med Exp Salud Publica*, Vol. 30(2), pp. 303-307, http://bit.ly/167Crsx.

Curioso, W.H., K. Pardo and L. Valeriano (2013b), "Uso de los establecimientos de salud del Ministerio de Salud del Perú, 2009-2011", *Rev Peru Med Exp Salud Publica*, Vol. 30(2), pp. 175-180, http://bit.ly/13gqPz1.

ECLAC – Economic Commission for Latin American and the Caribbean (2013), "Social Protection Systems in Latin America and the Caribbean", ECLAC, http://repositorio.cepal.org/bitstream/handle/11362/4049/S2013059_en.pdf?sequence=1.

Francke, P. (2013), "El Sistema Integral de Salud y los nuevos retos para la cobertura universal", http://www.paho.org/forocoberturagt2014/wp-content/uploads/2014/08/SERV-Estudio-UNICO-Peru.pdf.

IHME – Institute for Health Metrics and Evaluation (2011), "GDB Profile: Peru", IHME, http://www.healthdata.org/sites/default/files/files/country_profiles/GBD/ihme_gbd_country_report_peru.pdf.

INEI – National Statistics and Informatics Institute (2016), "Condiciones de vida en el Perú", retrieved from https://www.inei.gob.pe/media/MenuRecursivo/boletines/informe-tecnico-n02_condiciones-vida_octnovdic15.pdf.

INEI (2014), "Encuesta Nacional de Hogares", Instituto Nacional de Estadística e Informática.

Knaul, F. et al. (2011), "Household Catastrophic Health Expenditures: A Comparative Analysis of Twelve Latin American and Caribbean Countries", *Salud Pública de México*, Vol. 53, Suplemento 2, pp. 85-95, http://www.scielosp.org/pdf/spm/v53s2/05.pdf.

Málaga, R. et al. (2014), "Jóvenes que ni trabajan ni estudian: el caso peruano", Lima, Peru.

MINSA – Peruvian Ministry of Health (2016), "Instituciones Prestadoras de Servicios de Salud (IPRESS) en el marco del AUS", http://portales.susalud.gob.pe/web/cdi/ipress.

MINSA (2015), "Cuentas nacionales de salud Perú 1995-2012", retrieved from http://bvs.minsa.gob.pe/local/MINSA/3248.pdf.

MINSA (2011), "Recurson humanos en salud al 2011 – Evidencias para la toma de decisiones", http://www.bvsde.paho.org/texcom/cd046043/serieRHUS14.pdf?ua=1.

OECD (2017), *Monitoring Health System Performance in Peru: Data and Statistics,* OECD Publishing, Paris, http://dx.doi.org/10.1787/9789264282988-en.

OECD (2016), *OECD Health Statistics 2016*, OECD Publishing, Paris, http://dx.doi.org/10.1787/health-data-en.

OECD (2015), *Multi-dimensional Review of Peru: Volume 1. Initial Assessment*, OECD Development Pathways, OECD Publishing, Paris, http://dx.doi.org/10.1787/9789264243279-en.

OECD (2014a), *OECD Employment Outlook 2014*, OECD Publishing, Paris, http://dx.doi.org/10.1787/empl_outlook-2014-en.

OECD (2014b), *Society at a Glance 2014: OECD Social Indicators,* OECD Publishingb Paris, http://dx.doi.org/10.1787/soc_glance-2014-en.

Seinfeld, J. and N. Besich (2014), "Universal Health Coverage Assessment – Peru", Global Network for Health Equity.

UNDP – United Nations Development Programme (2015), "2015 Human Development Report (HDR) Work for Human Development", http://hdr.undp.org/sites/all/themes/hdr_theme/country-notes/PER.pdf.

UNDP (2009), "2009 Human Development Report (HDR) Human mobility and development, http://hdr.undp.org/sites/default/files/reports/269/hdr_2009_en_complete.pdf.

WHO – World Health Organization (2014), "Peru", http://www.who.int/substance_abuse/publications/global_alcohol_report/profiles/per.pdf?ua=1.

WHO (2006), *The World Health Report 2006: Working Together for Health*, Geneva.

World Bank (2016), "World Bank Open Data", http://data.worldbank.org/.

Chapter 2

Access and quality of health in Peru

Peru has made significant progress towards universal health coverage during the past decades. However, there are still challenges to overcome in order to provide accessible health care services of high quality to the whole population. Health care coverage needs to reach the uninsured population and stronger financial protection against out-of-pocket spending for health services should be established. Furthermore, increasing the health workforce density and distribution across Peru's geographical areas is a priority.

While improving access to health services, Peru ought also to focus on assuring and improving quality of care. A national framework on quality and standards, accompanied by robust quality assurance levers, will be key parts of this. The health information system could also be strengthened in order to monitor the performance of health providers within the different subsystems of the fragmented health care system, as well to help benchmark the overall performance of the health care system against other countries, building a good foundation of information for further policy making.

Introduction

Peru has made significant progress towards universal health coverage during the past decades. However, there are still challenges to overcome in order to provide accessible health care services of high quality to the whole population. The Peruvian health system faces challenges on several fronts, some of which are fundamental, notably the on-going need to achieve universal health coverage (UHC), and the vertical subsystems which present a major challenge to assuring quality and coverage for all Peruvians. Additionally, governance and steering of the system from the centre is weak, and weakened further by decentralisation of powers and competencies to the regions. Enhanced health system information – on costs, activities, and outcomes of care – is needed for more effective health system performance assessment and improvement.

As progress is made towards increased population health system coverage on paper, it will be essential to ensure that accessible and effective coverage for health care services of high quality is also achieved in practice. These are key questions that are further unpacked throughout this chapter, both in assessing to what degree Peru's health care system is set up so as to provide accessible and equitable, and effective and high-quality coverage, as well as recommendations to strengthen the system along these lines.

2.1. Access to health care in Peru

Despite good progress in the past decade, Peru still has a long way to go to achieve UHC. Policy to focus on pushing coverage much closer to 100% and well beyond the current 83%, needs to be stronger. Most strikingly, MINSA does not at present have a long-term strategy for achieving UHC, nor are there any established targets for increasing health coverage, nor an established horizon for when UHC should be achieved. Some other national actors, for instance SUSALUD, are involved in lobbying for UHC and monitoring progress on coverage. Nonetheless, this policy vacuum around the central issue of UHC is striking. This section further analyses the progress towards UHC and the accessibility of health care services for the Peruvian population.

Gaps in health system capacity and service use present a major challenge to access, and are variable across regions and subsystems

As illustrated in Chapter 1, a growing proportion of the Peruvian population has access to health care insurance and services. Health coverage has increased from 37% in 2004 to 73% in 2015 (OECD, 2015a; INEI, 2016), with latest estimates from SUSALUD indicated coverage of some 83%. There have also been commendable efforts to improve the package of coverage that SIS offers from an initially basic package; the Esperanza plan has also made a big difference to the accessibility of high-cost and longer term treatments, for example for cancer, for *Seguro Integral de Salud* (SIS) insured populations. There are signs, however, that shortages in available health services, and weaknesses in core infrastructure, are leading to significant problems with access to care.

Although the benefits of increasing health insurance have been fairly evenly distributed across rural and urban areas, coverage in some regions is clearly poorer than in others (Figure 2.1). in 2015, Puno and Tacna both had coverage below 70%, while La Libertat, Junin, Ica, and Pasco had coverage below 75%.

Figure 2.1. Health insurance coverage by region, 2015

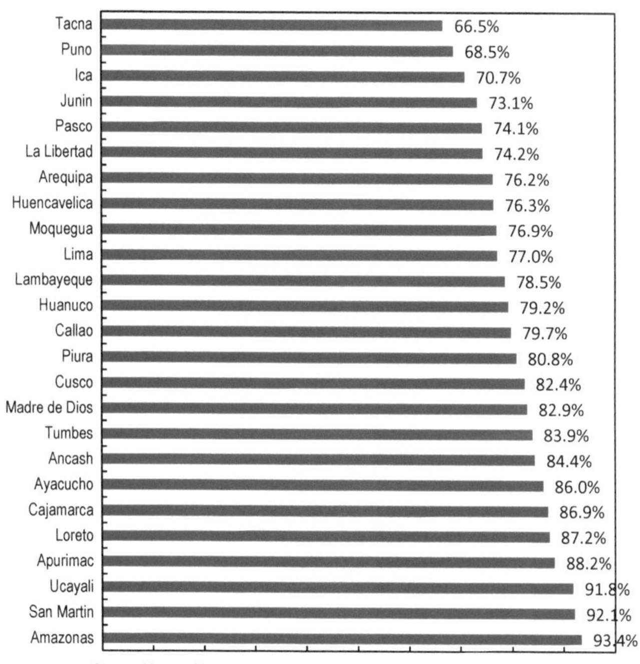

Source: Registro Nominal de Afiliados de SUSALUD.

There are key signs that the capacity of the health system, and capacity across subsystems, is not meeting demand. Long waiting times are reported, especially for EsSalud; as a result, many of the insured population under EsSalud have been reported as seeking care in MINSA facilities (9%), in private institutions (12%), as well as in pharmacies and drug stores (27%) (Seinfeld et al., 2013).

The distribution of infrastructure also varies by region, with hospital services overwhelmingly (97%) concentrated in urban areas, where populations tend to be richer. There are comparable numbers of hospitals owned by both EsSalud and MINSA. Table 2.1, from Seinfeld and Besich (2014), shows concentration indexes for utilisation of health services in Peru in 2012. Where the concentration has a positive value, the distribution of use is considered to benefit the richest populations (or, respectively, benefit the poorest if a negative value is observed). While these estimates are not adjusted for need, the concentration indexes for utilisation suggest that poorer populations may be facing some barriers to access.

Table 2.1. Concentration indexes for utilisation incidence of health service use in Peru, 2012

Type of service		Concentration index
Public facilities		**0.004**
Ministry of Health		-0.15
	Hospital	0.07
	Non-hospital	-0.21
Social security (EsSalud)		0.32
	Hospital	0.33
	Non-hospital	**0.28**
Private facilities		**0.33**
	Hospital	0.4
	Non-hospital	0.27
Total services		**0.09**
No services		-0.07

Source: Seinfeld, J. and N. Besich (2014), *Universal Health Coverage Assessment: Peru*, Global Network for Health Equity (GNHE).

The state of the hospital infrastructure and ambulatory facilities have, though, been called into question, and have seen little investment in recent decades, especially in poor areas (Vermeersch et al., 2014); in 2012 MINSA identified a set of 748 health centres that were to receive infrastructure investments from MINSA and regional governments. The utilisation of health services in Peru shows a pro-rich trend; only Ministry of Health non-hospital facilities are pro-poor, likely because they are in the great majority located in rural areas (Seinfeld and Besich, 2014).

Some population groups are furthermore particularly vulnerable to problems with accessing health care. Indigenous people, especially women, have been reported as experiencing difficulties in accessing health centres and, once accessed, can receive discriminatory treatment (OECD, 2015a). MINSA adopted the *Estrategia Sanitaria Nacional Salud de los Pueblos Indígenas* in 2009 in order to tackle the health inequalities faced by indigenous people, prioritising the Amazonian region. This plan aims to increase public health services for these regions, and to give greater respect to traditional practices and traditional medicine of indigenous people through an intercultural approach.

High out-of-pocket expenditure indicates that there are barriers to accessing effective care

As discussed in Chapter 1, private expenditure, and in particular out-of-pocket expenditure, is high in Peru. Out-of-pocket (OOP) expenditure represented 35% of total health expenditure in 2013, compared to the OECD average of 19.4% (World Bank, 2016; OECD, 2015b). The high OOP suggest that there is unmet need for effective insurance coverage in Peru, and likely suggests that total levels of public spending are insufficient.

At least a part of the high OOP can likely be explained by high levels of cost sharing for services, or services not covered by basic plans and thus necessitating OOP spend. In particular, high OOP spending both for medical consultations and pharmaceuticals are seen in MINSA services (see Figures 2.2 and 2.3).

Figure 2.2. Patient's expenditure on medical consultations by subsection, 2015

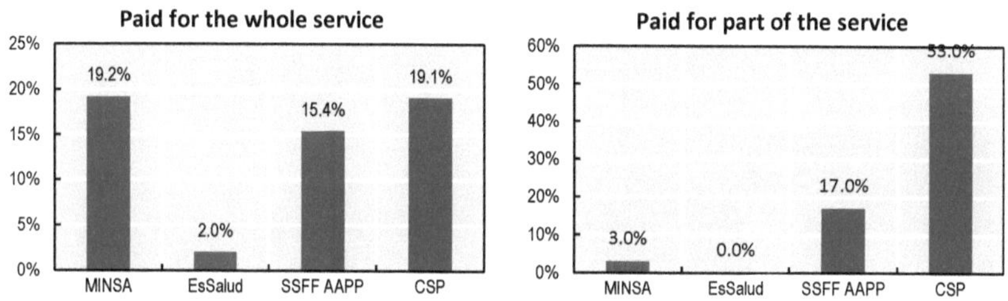

Source: SUSALUD, 2015; Instituto Nacional de Estadistica e Informatica-Encuesta Nacional de Satisfaccion de Usuarios en Salud 2015.

Figure 2.3. Patient's expenditure on medications prescribed in medical consultations, 2015

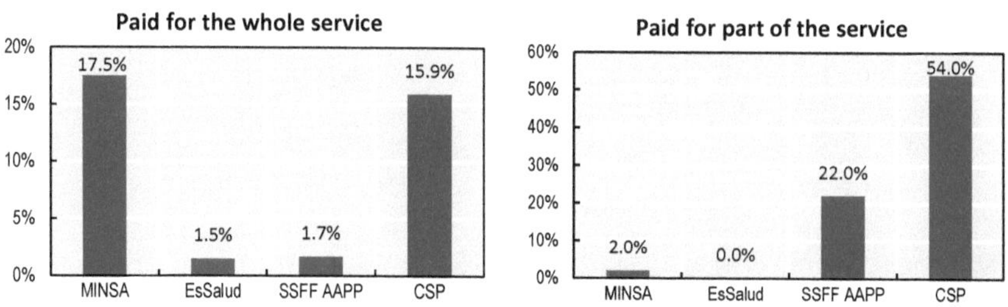

Source: SUSALUD, 2015; Instituto Nacional de Estadistica e Informatica-Encuesta Nacional de Satisfaccion de Usuarios en Salud 2015.

There appears to be a trend wherein Peruvians pay OOP for services, not just because of in-built cost sharing for services, but because either they are not satisfied with the services available to them under their insurance plans, or because they are uninsured. Of household spending on health, a reported 40.1% was for the purchase of drugs, 43.3% for the payment of private health services, and 11.6% for public services. This suggests that in addition to possibly routine cost sharing in health coverage plans, Peruvians are seeking out private care because it is easier to access, and/or thought to be of a higher quality. Similarly, the high OOP spend in MINSA could be explained in part by EsSalud insurees seeking care in MINSA facilities because of long waiting times, or perceived poorer services, in EsSalud facilities. Again, there are regional trends in the high OOP spending in MINSA facilities, which may be explained by the low capacity to meet demand, encouraging Peruvians to seek private care paid for OOP, or that there are higher rates of uninsured populations paying OOP in these areas (see also below).

While equity in health care access means that individuals receive health services according to need, equitable access to care also demands that patients can access appropriate care regardless of their capacity to pay for it. Financial protection is specifically important in lower socio-economic groups in order to reduce Catastrophic Health Expenditure (CHE) and Impoverishing Health Expenditure (IHE). When households are using more than 40% of non-food expenditures to pay for medical care, this is classed as catastrophic health expenditure. In Peru, 5% of households could be considered to have incurred CHE in 2012 (Seinfeld and Besich, 2014). CHE in Peru are much higher than the 0.73% in Costa Rica, although somewhat lower than the 6.4% reported in Chile (Knaul, 2011). In those households with catastrophic expenditure health spending accounted for an extremely high 80% of non-food household expenditure. Furthermore, Peruvian households can be understood to have been pushed into greater poverty from health spending, even when spending cannot be classed as catastrophic: in 2012, 7.5% of Peruvian households lived in extreme poverty – but, once household payments for health care were deducted from households, the poverty health count increased by 75 000 households, almost one full percentage point (Seinfeld and Besich, 2014). The degree to which that health spending still risks pushing Peruvian households into poverty is thus a real concern.

Peru presents health workforce shortages and imbalances in their geographical distribution

Density of physicians, nurses and obstetricians in Peru varies significantly across regions, creating large human resources gaps in the most vulnerable regions. On average there are 568 persons per doctor in Peru (compared to the OECD average of 303 persons per doctor in 2013 (OECD, 2015b), although the density of doctors across the population varies significantly. In Lima and Arequipa there are fewer than 350 inhabitants per doctor, while there are almost five times as many in Huancavelica, Huánuco, San Martín and Cajamarca. As seen in Figure 2.4, Peru not only has an uneven distribution of physicians, but the country also presents the lowest physician density among OECD countries (on average 1.7 physicians per 1 000 inhabitants, as compared to the OECD average of 3.3 per 1 000 inhabitants). As a consequence, a gap of some 16 000 specialists, including gynaecologists and obstetricians is reported.

A World Bank study about the health workforce in Peru found that even though health professionals are trained in both public and private universities, the majority do not end up working for public health providers and even less in rural and marginal areas. An initiative to level out the uneven geographical distribution of primary health care workforce has been through the Rural and Urban Marginal Health Service (*Servicio Rural y Urbano Marginal en Salud*, SERUMS). SERUMS are internships in rural or urban-marginal areas, with a normal duration of one year, which health professionals wanting to work in the public sector must enrol into. One year after completion of the SERUMS, however, it has been shown that only 25% of health professionals were working in the public sector, evidencing more attractive working conditions elsewhere. Moreover, only 10% of specialists were working in the public sector two years after completing their residencies (Jiménez et al., 2015).

The ratio of physicians and nurses to patients in Peru is reported as being quite significantly different between subsystems, although information on human resources by subsystems is not comprehensive due to the fragmented information systems. Big differences in payment across different subsystems within the Peruvian health care system exist. Starting salary for nurses is e.g. PEN 900 in MINSA and PEN 2 500 in EsSalud, despite MINSA's nurses taking care for the double of the number of patients. There are also significant salary differences across regions of the country, to the detriment of rural doctors specially. It appears that the market for health professionals in Peru offers health workers even more attractive salaries within the private sector, leading to difficulties in attracting and retaining high skilled health professionals in the public sector and thus, exacerbating human resource shortages in rural and remote areas served predominantly by public health providers.

Migration of health professionals to other countries is another important factor leading to shortages in health workforce in Peru. In 2010, 78% of medical students and 67% of nursing students said they wanted to practice their profession abroad after the completion of the university programme (Jiménez et al., 2015). Exactly how many professionals immigrate and emigrate, however, remains largely unknown due to the lack of quality of information on human resources for health.

Figure 2.4. Physician density by territorial level in OECD countries and in Peru, 2013 (or nearest year)

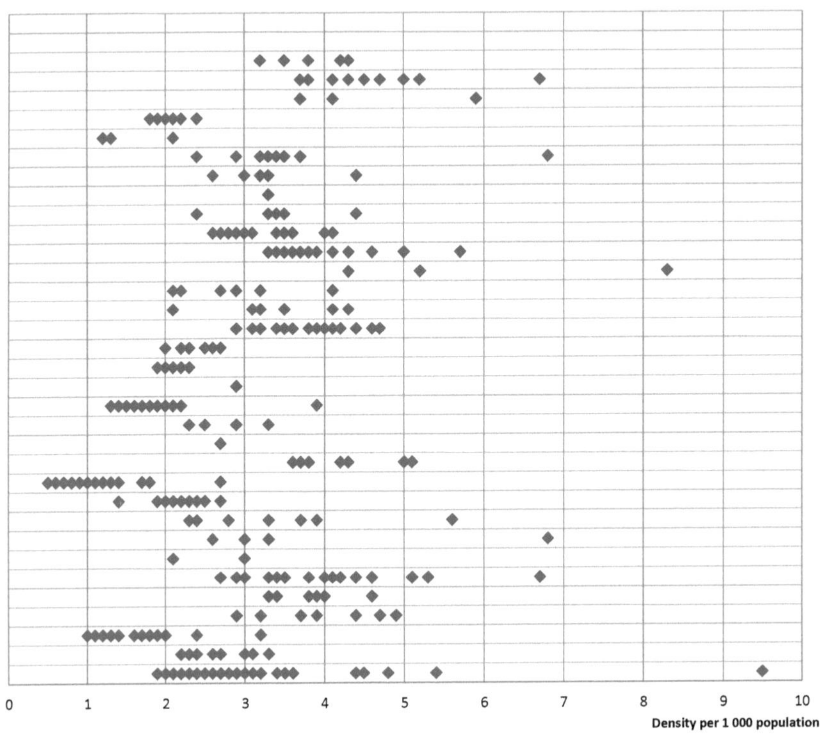

Source: OECD (2015), *Health at a Glance 2015: OECD Indicators,* OECD Publishing, Paris, http://dx.doi.org/10.1787/health_glance-2015-en; and MINSA (2015), "Información de Recursos Humanos en el Sector Salud: Perú 2014", retrieved from http://observatorio.inforhus.gob.pe/publicaciones/bibliograficos/libro21/polifoliar_2014.pdf.

Health system capacity, specifically in rural and remote areas, is a major concern in Peru. Data on type, amount and distribution of health professionals working in EsSalud or in the private sector should be reported to MINSA – but this is provided voluntarily and often not on a regular basis, thus limiting available information for comprehensive policy making. Shortages of health professionals are nevertheless recognised, and access to specialist services in rural areas is poor. In order to achieve UHC, national and regional workforce policies must therefore be strengthened, focussing on primary, as much as secondary and tertiary levels of care.

Strategies to increase primary care workforce, especially directed to the most vulnerable populations, started in 2007 and have been successful in extending the distribution of workforce and targeting it well. For secondary and tertiary care, the strategy has been to increase training places to around 2 000 per year to start covering up for the 16 000 shortage of specialists across the Peruvian health care system. The strategy has a regional approach and includes commencing to certify and license health specialists. Other initiatives undertaken are the development of specialist nurses and the quality development of existing workforce through the National School of Public Health. Through a three year education programme called *Programa Nacional de Formación en Salud Familiar y Comunitaria* (PROFAM), it is planned that 20 000 family medicine specialists will be trained by 2021. The first year of this programme is virtual, whereas the second and third year requires attendance to a university. So far, around 24 000 students have gone through the self-training first year.

The PROFAM programme follows the principles of the Universal Health Insurance Law (*Aseguramiento Universal en Salud*, AUS), as it is directed to basic health teams in primary health care settings (MINSA, 2011). The emphasis of the PROFAM programme during the second and third year of studies is integrated care networks for primary care. More universities however need to come into the training network in order to reach the full potential. Strategic training programmes are also available in mental health, public health, management and government, as well as in workforce management. Peru thus recognises that training must reflect strategic system priorities and there is a comprehensive and ambitious workforce strategy in place, led by the National School of Public Health.

There is a clear economic incentive for primary health care workers to be enrolled into PROFAM. As described in Chapter 1, there is a single national policy for MINSA services, made up of a basic payment and four additional components: i) performance payments; ii) regional bonus; iii) bonus for primary care workers or for hospital specialists; iv) bonus for additional responsibilities. Primary Health Care (*Atención Primaria de Salud*, APS) providers only get the bonus 3 (for primary care services) if they are enrolled into PROFAM. Bonuses get higher as each of the three years are completed. Likewise, hospital specialists have to renew their certification with a specialist college in order to receive their bonus, making it another incentive to improve quality of care. Additional bonuses for management competency are being discussed and would be important in order to enhance health care governance.

Health seeking behavior suggests acute problems in the capacity and quality of services

The expansion of health insurance coverage in Peru poses a real challenge to ensure effective coverage, i.e. coverage that guarantees actual access to high quality health services. According to IADB (2015), the rise in health insurance coverage has increased demand for health services and the provider network is not prepared to adequately respond to this rise in demand which poses a threat to effective insurance coverage. Self-reported health problems increased from 51.3% in 2004 to 61.5% in 2012 (MINSA, 2015a). Utilisation of health services (only at health facilities) of those reporting a health problem also increased (but to a lesser extent); from 31.0% to 32.7% between 2004 and 2012, which is an increase in demand (see Figure 2.5). Yet, the percentage of those who reported a health problem and chose to go to a pharmacy (self-medication) increased by from 26.3% to 29.3%.

Figure 2.5. Self-reported health problem and sought or did not seek formal care, 2002-12

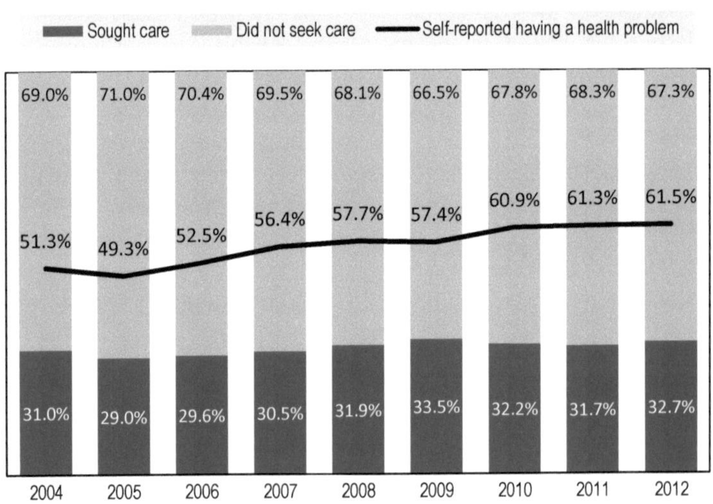

Source: Based on MINSA (2015), "Cuentas nacionales de salud Perú 1995-2012", retrieved from http://bvs.minsa.gob.pe/local/MINSA/3248.pdf.

When analysing insurance and access, MINSA concludes that those who have health insurance have scarcely chosen its corresponding provider network (MINSA, 2015a). They find a limited correlation between having insurance and being able to draw upon its benefits when the person self-reports a health problem. This lack of correlation is implied by the choice of seeking care and the choice of providers. Figure 2.6 shows the health care seeking behaviour of EsSalud and SIS beneficiaries in 2004, 2012, and 2014. Among EsSalud beneficiaries who declared having a health problem, those who sought care at a health facility (formal care) fell from 52.4% to 44.7%. Also, the choice of provider is shifting away from EsSalud's provider network towards private providers and going straight to the pharmacy is increasing. The case of SIS beneficiaries is similar: demand for formal care fell and the choice of provider is shifting from the public network towards private providers and pharmacies. Both the decrease in demand for formal care and the shift towards private providers or pharmacy (self-medication) show a decline in the effectiveness of both EsSalud and SIS.

Figure 2.6. Health care seeking behaviour, 2004, 2012 and 2014

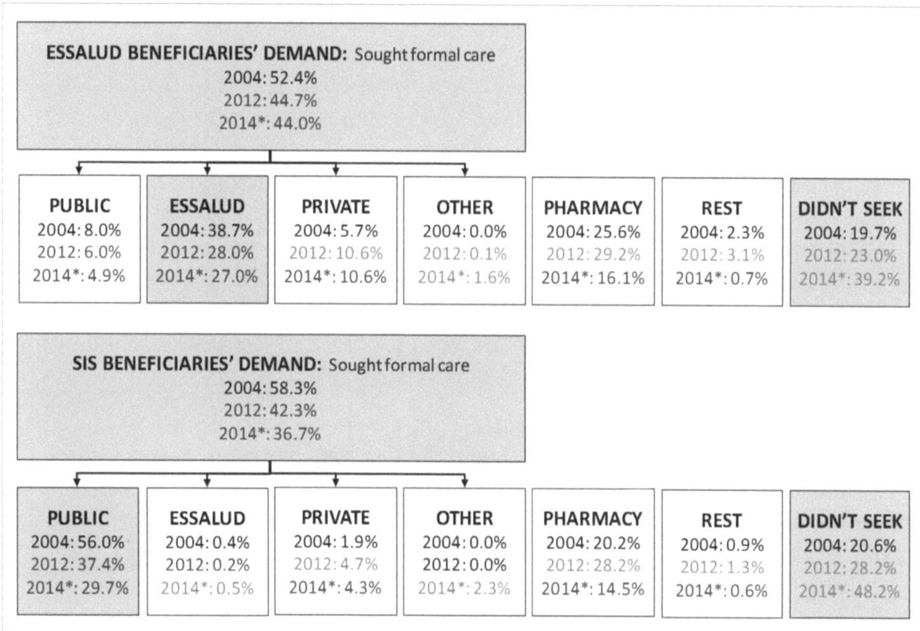

Note: The ENAHO survey allows for several options with regards to the place that was chosen to seek care.

*: Differences between 2004/2012 and 2014 may be due to differences in methods to calculate choices.

Source: Based on MINSA (2015), "Cuentas nacionales de salud Perú 1995-2012 », retrieved from http://bvs.minsa.gob.pe/local/MINSA/3248.pdf for 2004 and 2012, own calculations for 2014 using ENAHO.

The design of the questions in this MINSA survey (MINSA, 2015a) is somewhat misleading. For instance, little scope is given for declaring that care was unavailable or unsatisfactory in possible responses. Choices instead include, as explanation for what responders did not seek care, "did not have time", "chose to self-medicate", or "did not consider the problem to require care". These responses do little to unpack the reasons behind these choices not to seek help; for instance, high cost of formal care making self-medication a more affordable option, or that the responders felt they did not have time to access care given the long waits involved. Nonetheless, some of the responses are indicative of a broad trend in which Peruvians do not seek health care, even when experiencing a health problem.

In 2014, of those declaring having only EsSalud coverage, 56.3% declared having a non-chronic health problem in the last four weeks. From this group, more people decided not to seek formal care (56.7%), than those who did (43.3%). EsSalud coverage is provided through its own network of health facilities at no additional cost for its beneficiaries. Of EsSalud beneficiaries who declared having a health problem and who sought care, 61.4% did so at an EsSalud provider, 11.1% chose a public provider and the remaining 27.6% chose other providers (in the last two cases with out-of-pocket payments). This shows that EsSalud is not providing an effective coverage to almost two out of five of its beneficiaries who are choosing other providers and paying out-of-pocket. In fact, although the main reason not to seek care was that people declaring a health problem did not consider the problem to require care (36.6%), the next most important reason is because they prefer to self-medicate (24%) followed by because they did not have time (16.9%).

In the case of SIS beneficiaries for the same year, 61.9% declared having a non-chronic health problem in the last four weeks, more than in the case of EsSalud. As in the case of EsSalud, SIS provides coverage using the public network of health facilities. Among those declaring a health problem, 63.7% decided not to seek formal care, and only 36.3% did seek care. Among those who sought formal care 80.9% did so at a public provider, 1.4% chose an EsSalud provider and the remaining 17.7% chose another provider. In the case of SIS, its beneficiaries are more likely to choose a public provider, but a larger proportion chooses not to seek formal care. SIS beneficiaries also declare the main reason not to seek care to be because they did not consider the problem to require care (29.0%), but, unlike EsSalud, the next most important reason is that they do not have time to seek care (16.2%) followed by they prefer to use homemade remedies (15.8%) or they self-medicate (15.6%).

Peruvians perceive that the accessibility of health care services is poor, and has not been improving

Looking at health-seeking behaviour by Peruvians insured under the different subsystems, again suggests that even insured populations are not receiving effective care, and that perceived quality of care is poor. Effective coverage is being damaged by poor health insurance coverage, by insufficient capacity to meet demand, by poor quality of available care, or by all three.

Many Peruvians report being unhappy with the level of accessibility of their health services, including in comparison to other nations in the region (Figure 2.7). The Gallup World Poll asks individuals whether they think that services in their country are accessible to them, regardless of economic situation. The share of Peruvians who believed that anyone could access health care increased between 2006 and 2010, from 35% to 45%, in line with the expansion of the SIS. From 2010, however, opinions on the accessibility of health care deteriorated, although did see a slight improvement in 2014.

Figure 2.7. Perceptions of the accessibility of health care services in Peru and neighbouring countries, 2006-14

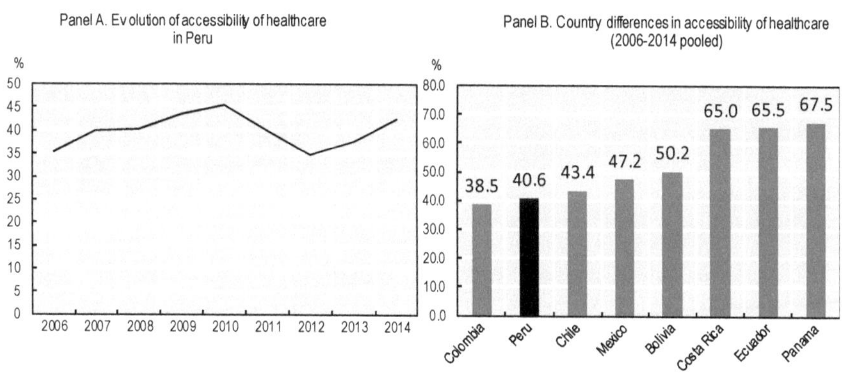

Note: Data for "perceptions of accessibility of health care" show the percentage of people responding "yes" to the question "Are health care services in this country accessible to any person who needs then, regardless of their economic situation, or not?"

Source: Gallup organisation (2015), Gallup World Monitor (database).

2.2. Promoting equitable access to effective health care in Peru

This section provides opportunities to strengthen the Peruvian health care infrastructure and workforce in order to reach the uninsured and vulnerable populations and thus promote equitable access to health care services.

Reaching Peru's uninsured populations

In order to reach UHC in Peru, which should be an urgent policy priority, the remaining 17% of the population without insurance must be insured. At current estimated increase rates, some 20% will remain uninsured by the end of this decade. Decisive action is needed to accelerate the pace at which Peru moves towards UHC. At present however, the two main insurers do not seem to convince the uninsured to voluntarily buy their coverage, which translates into the inefficient alternative of OOP expenditures to receive care and makes achievement of the UHC goal very difficult if not impossible.

One option to achieve UHC would be to expand the scope of SIS. SIS has experimented with different schemes to expand its coverage to the non-poor population without health insurance, albeit with little success. As described in Chapter 1, SIS created the semi-subsidised regime for people with low ability to pay in 2007. In addition, in 2013, a new attempt to include non-poor populations was made through SIS Entrepreneurs, which affiliated independent workers who signed up for the New Unique Simplified Regime. Affiliation to SIS is automatic through this mechanism and no additional payments are required besides paying taxes. According to SIS, in September 2015, the number of beneficiaries in schemes for people with low ability to pay was 241 880 which represents only 1.5% of all of SIS beneficiaries. An approximate 9 million still have no insurance.

Another option would be to develop, or encourage the development of, private health insurance packages that would be attractive to Peruvians who do not qualify for the SIS as their incomes are too high, but who are in informal employment, or are self-employed, and therefore do not qualify for EsSalud coverage.

There are some country examples that Peru could follow, including some OECD countries – notably Korea, and Turkey – where UHC has been achieved relatively recently, and relatively rapidly. The remarkable achievements of Colombia in achieving UHC, though, are perhaps most pertinent as an international example to follow. Colombia should also be seen as an example to follow in reducing the financial burden of health care for households (see Box 2.1).

Box 2.1. Achieving UHC in Colombia

Colombia's record in extending health insurance and health services to its population is impressive. In 1990, around one in six of the population had health insurance. Now, nearly 97% do, with greatest expansion occurring amongst the poorer households. Likewise, in 1993 out-of-pocket spending made up 52% of total national expenditure on health. By 2006, this had fallen to less than 15%, and remains one of the lowest figures in the region.

Through the *Ley 100* in 1993, Colombia restructured the health care system. A contributory regime (CR) and a publicly subsidised regime (SR) was created. Individuals obliged to affiliate through the CR are those with employment contracts, people receiving a pension or self-employed individuals earning at least the minimum wage (in practice, relatively few). Colombians' most frequent contact with the health system is via bodies called EPS and IPS. The *Entidades Promotoras de Salud* (EPS, health insurance agencies) are responsible for organising and guaranteeing the provision of health services included in the defined benefit-basket for their enrolled populations. They are also expected to manage population health risks. EPS are required to recruit health service providers to guarantee the access for activities to health promotion, disease prevention, and care at all levels including rehabilitation. The *Instituciones Prestadoras de Salud* (IPS), on the other hand, are health care provider institutions such as hospitals, and clinics.

Within the Colombian health care system, a managed competition model exists. Individuals enrol with an EPS of their choice and, at times of health care need, access an IPS of their choice within their EPS network. By law, vertical integration between EPS and IPS is limited to 30% of the insurer's total spend.

Health system funding comes from a variety of sources; mainly employee and employer payroll contributions for the CR; and national and local tax revenues, as well as cross-subsidisation from the CR in the case of SR. FOSYGA (*Fondo de Seguridad y Garantía*) is the institution in charge of pooling health funds accruing to CR, whereas funds for the SR are pooled at the national and (maily) local levels. EPS receive their revenues through a capitated payment (*Unidad de Pago por Capitación*, UPS) per enrollee, with some adjustment for geographic, demographic and – to a lesser extent – epidemiologic factors. In 2008, the Constitutional Court ruled that the benefits package in the CR and SR regimes should be equalised for children aged under 18 years, within a year. At the same time, the Court required a programme and a timetable for the gradual and sustainable unification of the benefits packages for the rest of the population. This ruling was carried out in 2012. Additional funds were found to meet these commitment, and equal per capita allocations were achieved at the beginning of 2015.

Source: OECD (2015), *OECD Reviews of Health Systems: Colombia 2016*, OECD Publishing, Paris, http://dx.doi.org/10.1787/9789264248908-en.

Achieving UHC is within reach for Peru, but in order to do so, and regardless of the approach chosen, high-level commitment is needed. There must be political will to make UHC a reality, backed with a national plan for implementation, necessarily accompanied by fairly significant financial investments. Peru is in need of an Agenda for National Action on Health, which brings in all actors to sign-up, to bring more detail and actionability to the for the moment relatively vague ambition of UHC. This agenda should have a focus on providing good coverage for a well-defined basket of benefits rather than providing shallow coverage for any service with high patient cost-sharing. Financial sustainability also needs to be built into the system, including by exploring options to broaden revenue sources and prioritise use of resources. Reforms should focus on strengthening primary care, as well as making better use of data through developing more advanced and integrated information systems throughout all service delivery subsystems in the country.

Peru should focus on assuring effective health services for vulnerable populations

In pursuing UHC, Peru should make equity a priority. Poorer rural groups, particularly in boarder areas and the Amazon region, and indigenous populations, are still reported as having particular unmet needs. As well as considering equity dimensions when increasing UHC – again, Colombia is a country to follow here, where health insurance affiliation increased most rapidly amongst poorer quintiles following the 1993 reform – equity of access should be considered when developing health care capacity. The relationship established between Peru and Colombia, under the framework of the European Union's EUROsociAL, to support Peru in following Colombia's successful experience in establishing an Observatory for Measuring Inequalities and Analysis of Equity in Health (ODES), is encouraging (FIIAPP, 2015).

To some extent, access to services for vulnerable populations could be expected to improve if the total capacity of the health system increased (see the following section). However, given the challenges of expanding capacity in remote and rural areas, concerted attention should be given to such vulnerable groups as well.

Box 2.2 Rural and remote health in Australia

In order to increase the capability of rural and remote health, Peru could learn from experiences in Australia. Workforce innovation has been embraced in Australia, including strategies that changed the scopes of practice, flying specialists in and out of remote areas, and offering doctors financial incentives to move to areas of need. Australia developed a National Strategic Framework for Rural and Remote Health in order to address the complexities of delivering health services in the most remote areas of the country. The framework aims to promote a national approach to policy, planning, design and delivery of health services in rural and remote communities. The framework cites wide variations between rural and remote communities and as a consequence, a "one size fits all" approach cannot be applied throughout rural and remote Australia. The framework therefore encourages health service planning and delivery that recognises the need to develop solutions to meet the unique needs of local populations.

Goals

Rural and remote communities will have:

1. improved access to appropriate and comprehensive health care
2. effective, appropriate and sustainable health care service delivery
3. an appropriate, skilled and well-supported health workforce
4. collaborative health service planning and policy development
5. strong leadership, governance, transparency and accountability

Outcome areas

The framework lists objectives and strategies under five outcome areas. These are:

1. access
2. service models and models of care
3. health workforce
4. collaborative partnerships and planning at the local level
5. strong leadership, governance, transparency and performance

Source: OECD (2015), *OECD Reviews of Health Care Quality: Australia 2015: Raising Standards*, OECD Publishing, Paris, http://dx.doi.org/10.1787/9789264233836-en.

In particular, efforts need to be made to ensure that the basic health needs of remote and rural populations in Peru are met; indications of infectious disease rates including dengue and chikungunya are extremely worrying. In terms of ensuring effective protection from infectious diseases, it seems clear that a central role is needed. The fact that rates of some diseases have risen since the decentralisation of control over public and preventive health to regional governments is disquieting, and suggests that either governments do not have the skills to deliver effective preventive services, or that they are not making prevention a political or financial priority. It seems that there is a need for MINSA to play a stronger role, which might include some of the following:

- MINSA setting clear standards that all regions must meet in terms of basic provision, which can be measured against indicators such as incidence of priority diseases. Moving towards a broader focus on public health, regional performance on obesity (adult and child), smoking rates, drinking and drug use, could be included in standards and systematically reported indicators. Regions likely need greater support to build knowledge and skills around effective health prevention and promotion.
- Peru also may need to consider a ruling that a certain percentage of regional health funds are spent on preventive health activity, as was undertaken in Mexico (OECD, 2016b).
- That prevention and health promotion responsibilities be re-centralised, to either MINSA or a third party organisation. Even while OECD countries are showing a trend towards decentralisation in their health systems, which can have clear benefits, the retention of core public health functions at the central level is not uncommon. This approach could be taken in Peru – where decentralisation seems to have been popular with citizens – and where a balance could be struck between popular decentralisation, and safety concerns around rates of infectious diseases. A good example for Peru to follow could be the approach of national programmes undertaken in Mexico (see Box 2.3).

Box 2.3. Public health and health promotion activities in the Mexican health system

The Under-Secretariat for Prevention and Health Promotion within the Mexican Ministry of Health manages 35 national programmes, with a budget of MXN 3 810 million in 2014 (EUR 213 million, USD 260 million). Some of the most important programmes delivered include:

- *Epidemiological surveillance:* all public hospitals and the larger private hospitals participate in a national surveillance system, intended to rapidly and effectively identify emerging epidemiological trends.
- *Community-oriented public health programmes:* working in partnership with local communities and municipal authorities, these programmes aim to create healthy schools, parks, markets and other public spaces. Specific actions include eliminating hazards to health such as mosquito reservoirs and building safe, welcoming spaces to encourage people to exercise.
- *Vaccination programmes:* free and universal vaccination programmes have led to the eradication or control of several infectious diseases such as poliomyelitis, diphtheria and neonatal tetanus. Several initiatives maintain population coverage, including Vaccination Days, National Health Weeks, and surges of activity during outbreaks (such as contact training).
- *Control of dengue fever and other vector-borne diseases:* again working closely with local communities and municipal authorities, these programmes aim to prevent and eradicate sites where disease-carrying vectors may reside. Education and training programmes, oriented towards local communities, are offered.
- *Health protection during outbreaks and natural disasters:* Mexico's location makes it prone to torrential rains, hurricanes and other natural disasters. Over recent decades, a number of health protection programmes have been established to anticipate and react promptly to such emergencies. These include surveillance, mobile health units, temporary refuges and activities to prevent outbreaks of diarrhoeal or respiratory infections where large numbers of people are temporarily housed together. Mental health services are also offered.

Source: OECD (2016), *OECD Reviews of Health Systems: Mexico 2016*, OECD Publishing, Paris, http://dx.doi.org/10.1787/9789264230491-en.

Key gaps in infrastructure need to be closed

As technical coverage is extended with the move towards UHC, it will be essential to ensure that there is capacity within the health system to meet first, the increasing populations looking to access care, and second, the changing health needs of the population. The volume of health services will need to be increased, and when increasing health services Peru should look forward and anticipate the epidemiological transition towards chronic disease that can already be observed.

As discussed, clear evidence suggests that the health system is not meeting demand for care. This can be seen particularly in the low rate at which Peruvians report that health services are accessible (Figure 2.7), as well as in the rate at which Peruvians are prepared to pay OOP for their care. OOP spending by Peruvians accessing care in facilities not owned by their own health insurance subsystem suggests that there is some scope for the *intercambio* (service exchange agreements) to have an impact on improving access (see further in this section). At present, however, *intercambios* seem to be used only in a very limited way.

Improvements in physical access to health services have been implemented with investment in infrastructure and equipment for health service and hospital networks. However, according to Bambarén and Alatrista (2015), the infrastructure gap for primary health care is estimated at USD 478 million, which includes 101 new health centres, 180 new basic health units, and 5 new basic hospitals. They estimated the hospital infrastructure gap comparing the number of beds per 1 000 population with other LAC countries. Peru had 1.5 beds per 1 000 population, while Argentina, Chile and Brazil, for example, had 4.7, 2.2 and 2.1 respectively in 2013. In OECD countries hospital beds were as low as 1.6 in Mexico or as high as 13.3 in Japan (OECD, 2016a). It is important to note that these investment gap estimates do not consider other variables such as increased demand due to expansion of insurance coverage, socio-economic determinants of the demand for services, changes in demand due to the epidemiological transition, productive efficiency of health facilities or potential supply. Not considering these factors indicate that the infrastructure gap could be different in the future, although it is unclear whether it could be worse.

Strengthening the supply of health services is a priority and in line with this goal MINSA has an initiative to improve the response capacity of 748 health facilities – denominated strategic facilities – to strengthen primary health care. In 2015, MINSA reached an agreement with regional governments to establish 170 provincial strategic hospitals, 22 regional hospitals and 12 national hospitals by 2021 (El Comercio, 2015b). But, the implementation process of these investments has been slow, due to the pre-investment requirements and also the actual infrastructure investment.

Also, when Madueño et al. (2003) estimated the supply and demand gaps for the health sector they estimated a utilisation index based that measured utilisation relative to the production capacity for 2003. They estimated an utilisation index of 62% production capacity. But, they assumed productive efficiency, which is a very strong assumption, because it is unlikely all if any health facility was operating at full productive efficiency. But this helps highlight the management problems in the use of available resources, because if the sector were productively efficient it would be able to provide all necessary services.

Another challenge to improve management and hence efficiency of providers is caused by the fragmented financial flows towards public providers – divided into several operators including SIS, regional and local governments. An effort to improve efficiency and the sustainability of health insurance would be the implementation of cross-sector purchases of services. Initially, SIS could only purchase services from public providers and EsSalud could not buy services from other providers nor sell its services to SIS beneficiaries. Allowing SIS to purchase services from EsSalud providers, and EsSalud to purchase services from public providers, reduces the health care fragmentation and lead to a more efficient use of the supply of care. Cross-sector purchasing of services is a mechanism for service integration; something badly needed in a highly fragmented health system.

SIS signed its first cross-sector contracts (denominated as service exchange agreements) with Lima's Municipality Solidarity Hospitals (*Hospitales de la Solidaridad*, SISOL) in 2011 and later with EsSalud. Table 2.2 shows the latest statistics of SIS contracts with other providers. It includes payments SIS makes for emergency services and service contracts to provide health services to SIS beneficiaries (since mid-2013), haemodialysis (mid-2014), diagnosis and treatment of refractive errors for children in primary school (mid-2014), and purchase of drugs and medicines from pharmacies (September 2015). The total amount spent has increased in the last three years, as well as its participation in SIS' total budget.

Table 2.2. SIS purchases of services from providers outside its network, 2013-15

	2013	2014	2015
Service exchange			
SISOL	5,628,677.72	12,733,512.94	9,541,558.53
EsSalud	223,213.96	88,390.40	329,540.03
Service contracts	39,854.88	137,580.10	2,546,456.77
Emergency services	0	780,661.60	7,809,562.75
Total	**5,891,746.56**	**13,740,145.04**	**20,227,118.08**
Budget	931,549,786.00	1,240,273,080.00	1,558,022,216.00
Purchases of services/Budget	0.63	1.11	1.3

Source: SIS and MEF.

Increasing health workforce and leveling out geographical imbalances in human resource distribution

The Peruvian health care system has insufficient funds to increase workforce and level out the geographical distribution throughout the country as fast as needed. The academic capacity to increase health care workforce in Peru is furthermore weak and uneven across geographical regions. Within this concern, there are many opportunities for Peru to learn from the experiences of OECD countries. Peru could implement interventions that have been experienced by OECD countries as presented in an OECD report on health workforce policies (OECD, 2016c), such as:

- influencing the choice of practice location at the end of the training period through interventions at different points in the *medical education* process. These include the selection of students in entry to medical schools and the design and geographic distribution of post-graduate clinical training programmes (see Box 2.4 and Box 2.5).
- offering various types of *financial incentives* to attract more physicians in underserved areas, starting from providing special scholarship at entry to medical schools and/or post-graduate clinical training (possible combined with return-of-service obligation), to one-off payments to doctors to support their installation in underserved areas, to recurrent payments and bonuses to recruit and retain them in underserved areas (see Box 2.6).
- regulating which type of physicians is allowed to work where. Regulation can be put in place at the time of entry to post-graduate clinical training (such as public service obligations) or in restricting the choice of practice location when new doctors want to set up a first practice (Box 2.7).
- redesigning health service delivery to help to improve the working conditions of doctors in underserved areas (e.g., by creating group practices to overcome the isolation of solo practice) and/or promote the use of innovative health service delivery to provide adequate level of access with fewer physicians (e.g. through telemedicine) or shifting some health service provision from physicians to other health care providers (Box 2.8).

Box 2.3. Student selection to counter geographical workforce imbalances in Australia

In Australia, the federal government offers three medical school placement schemes, although the third one (the MRBS) has been closed to new entrants in 2016. Under the commonwealth-supported places schemes, students pay part of the medical degree and the remainder is subsidised by the government, with no conditions attached. Both the Bonded Medical Places (BMP) scheme and the Medical Rural Bonded Scholarship (MEBS) scheme require students to repay the cost to the government of their place (BMP) or their scholarship (MRBS) if they break the contract. In the case of the MRBS scheme, physicians may not be able to have access to the Medicare schedule for up to 12 years.

Under the BMP scheme, the Australian Government offers an additional 700 medical training placement per year (rising to 800 from 2017). Students have to sign a deed of agreement with the government to work in a district of physician shortage for a period equal to the length of training. More than 4 500 participants had such an agreement in 2013, but only one had commenced his/her return-of-service obligation and three had chosen to repay the cost of their education. In contrast, students offered the MRBS scheme received substantial financial aid and signed a contract with the government to work in a rural or remote area for six years after completing specialist training. There were 100 placements available each year. Since 2001, more than 1 200 students participated in this programme but only 50 have started the return-of-service obligation period. The MRBS scheme was closed to new from 2016, with these 100 medical places being transferred to the BMP scheme.

Source: OECD (2016), *Health Workforce Policies in OECD Countries: Right Jobs, Right Skills, Right Places*, OECD Health Policy Studies, OECD Publishing, Paris, http://dx.doi.org/10.1787/9789264239517-en.

Box 2.4. Policies aimed at training institutions to address shortage of physicians in Norway

In Norway, the Univerity of Tromsø's school of medicine was established in 1972 in northern Norway to address a chronic shortage of physicians. When the school was established, a quota of 25% was reserved for students from northern Norway in the belief that a greater percentage of these students would remain there after graduation; this share was increased to 50% in 1979 and 60% in 1998. As a result, the number of medical graduates with a north-Norwegian origin increased from 41% in the period from 1979 to 1988, to 57% in the period from 1996 to 2001. Research has shown that most medical graduates from the University of Tromsø do remain in northern Norway. Of the medical students who graduated between 1979 and 1988, 56% continued to work in northern Norway, though this fell to 51% for graduates from 1996 to 2001. There is also evidence that the likelihood of graduates remaining in northern Norway is particularly high if they are of northern Norwegian origin. Among the University of Tromsø graduates from 1996 to 2001, 75% of physicians with northern Norwegian origin chose to practise there, while only 19% of physicians with a southern Norwegian origin remained after graduation.

Source: OECD (2016), *Health Workforce Policies in OECD Countries: Right Jobs, Right Skills, Right Places*, OECD Health Policy Studies, OECD Publishing, Paris, http://dx.doi.org/10.1787/9789264239517-en.

Box 2.5 Financial incentives to level out geographical imbalances in health workforce in Canada

In the Canadian province of British Columbia, the Rural Retention Programme grants physicians an annual bonus based on "isolation points" determined by the existence of other physicians in surrounding areas and the community's geographical characteristics. In 2008, 144 communities were entitled to grant physicians an allowance and 1 568 physicians benefitted in 2007-08.

Financial incentives can also aim to encourage doctors to postpone retirement. In Canada's rural areas in Alberta, annual bonuses range from CAD 4 000 (EUR 2 800, USD 3 100) after five years of practice, rising to CAD 10 000 (EUR 7 000, USD 7 700) after 26 years.

Source: OECD (2016), *Health Workforce Policies in OECD Countries: Right Jobs, Right Skills, Right Places*, OECD Health Policy Studies, OECD Publishing, Paris, http://dx.doi.org/10.1787/9789264239517-en.

Box 2.6. Regulation of physician practice location in Germany

In Germany, the number of practice permits for ambulatory care physicians in a specific region is limited, based on a national service delivery quota. Physicians need to obtain a practice permit to be reimbursed by the statutory health insurance. The number of these permits is controlled by the National Association of Statutory Health Insurance Physicians (NASHIP) through its 17 state associations. The NASHIP is the self-regulated organisation of about 120 000 physicians practising under the statutory health insurance.

It is mandated by the government to guarantee medical service coverage of the population based on a quota agreed within the self-administration of the German health care system. The service coverage is measured based on the ration between physicians and inhabitants in each of the 395 planning regions. For GPs, 100% coverage is achieved when the ratio of GP to inhabitant reaches 1:1 617. If the coverage of a region exceed 110%, no further permits are issued.

Source: OECD (2016), *Health Workforce Policies in OECD Countries: Right Jobs, Right Skills, Right Places*, OECD Health Policy Studies, OECD Publishing, Paris, http://dx.doi.org/10.1787/9789264239517-en.

Box 2.7. Group practices within health workforce in France

In France, the *Maisons de Santé Pluridisciplinaires* (MSP) were introduced in 2007. They differ from other forms of group practices because they allow physicians and other health professionals to jointly run group practices while remaining self-employed. MSPs are either entirely financed by the health professionals, or receive subsidies from various sources, such as the European Union, governments and the French health insurance. By 2012, 235 MSPs had been set up in France and another 450 were planned, with 80% of them located in rural areas. MSPs lead to better work conditions and greater accessibility for patients. In a survey in France-Comté and Bourgogne, 71 GPs in nine MSPs reported a weekly workload of 46 hours compared to 52-60 hours in other practices. MSP opening hours were better with an average of 5.5 opening days/week, and 11.5 opening hours per day. The quality of follow-up care for diabetes patients was also improved.

Source: OECD (2016), *Health Workforce Policies in OECD Countries: Right Jobs, Right Skills, Right Places,* OECD Health Policy Studies, OECD Publishing, Paris, http://dx.doi.org/10.1787/9789264239517-en.

New programmes focussing on the development of primary care workforce could moreover be developed in Peru, as well as a revision and improvement of existing ones both in public and private universities. Shorter, community based courses could be included in these programmes and these should be linked to a high employability after completion. Furthermore, it is important that new programmes for primary care health professionals be located in local regions so that students are close to their residencies and are incentivised to stay in their regions also after completion of the training.

In order to achieve better contracts and retain more professionals, MINSA should strategically review compensation mechanisms. The health workforce payment system needs to be based on more generous and consistent salary scale, with additional bonuses as appropriate. These should include incentives for the whole workforce team, and prioritise primary care and regional and remote areas. In order to address geographic imbalances in the distribution of health workforce, Peru has implemented the SERUMS programme to promote rotations of doctors from urban to rural and marginal-urban areas, as earlier described. This programme should nonetheless be complemented with retention strategies in order to attract professionals to continue working in rural and marginal-urban areas also after the completion of the SERUMS. Studies that include job aspirations and expectations should be included in order to assess possible retention strategies.

The distribution of health care workforce by subsector is difficult to obtain due to the fragmented information systems among the different health insurers in Peru. Strategic alliances among key actors on workforce information would need to be developed in order to integrate human resource information. This would be an important step for policy purposes, since it would allow a comprehensive picture of the human resource distribution and thus facilitate strategic planning and decision-making.

2.3. Quality of care in the Peruvian health system

In OECD countries, quality issues have gained importance in recent years as governments and the public increasingly focus on what is being delivered in exchange for major public investments in health care. The quality of care delivered by health services is crucial to making sure that health care is effective, and helps deliver good outcomes for citizens. Key building blocks of a country's quality of care architecture help make sure that care is effective and safe. OECD assessment of the quality of care architecture for health systems takes stock of these building blocks, identified in Table 2.3. Following the broad tenets of this framework, the effectiveness of Peru's basic quality architecture can be assessed.

Table 2.3. A typology of health care policies that influence health care quality

Policy	Examples
Health system design	Accountability of actors, allocation of responsibilities, legislation
Health system input (professionals, organisations, technologies)	Professional licensing, accreditation of health care organisations, quality assurance of drugs and medical devices
Health system monitoring and standardisation of practice	Measurement of quality of care, national standards and guidelines, national audit studies and reports on performance
Improvement (national programmes, hospital programmes and incentives)	National programmes on quality and safety, pay for performance in hospital care, examples of improvement programmes within institutions

Health system design: governance and legislative framework

As described in Chapter 1, Peru has a vertically integrated and decentralised health care system, with five main health care insurers – MINSA, EsSalud, the army and the police forces and the private sector –, and each scheme owns and operates its own clinics and hospitals. Following the decentralisation reform in Peru, supervision and management of health services, and financial resources, was transferred to regional and local governments, primarily to improve the efficiency and to make health services more responsive to local needs (see also Chapter 3). There are a number of legislative provisions, which seek to assure that health insurers and providers deliver effective care.

However, there are already some signs that the dual fragmentation of the system – vertically by subsystem, and horizontally to regions – is causing problems for quality of care. In terms of regional decentralisation, the persistence of high infectious disease burden and diminishing vaccination coverages (as described in Chapter 1) is a warning sign that regional authorities are not fully competent to provide sufficiently good care for populations. Low user satisfaction and readiness of Peruvians to seek care outside of their insurance-covered providers, and/or pay for care out-of-pocket, suggest that there are variable problems with quality within the subsystems.

Quality assurance of health care providers, health care workforce, pharmaceuticals, and medical devices

Minimum standards for quality are under the control of MINSA, and depend on accreditation by MINSA. Although a model of accreditation is directed by SUSALUD, no national accreditation programme for hospitals exists. A new accreditation model is nevertheless being elaborated. Beyond this, SIS has a quality control system, and 20 items of audit. Services can be put under special supervision or have their provider contract cancelled. There are moreover 16 existing standards (for HIV, leprosy, vaccinations, cancer, malnutrition etc.), but they are disease-specific, and not exhaustive.

Medical professionals working in the health system are regulated under a number of legislative provisions:

- the General Health Law, Law No. 26842, of 9.7.1997, Article 22, which sets out that "to perform own professional activities of medicine, dentistry, pharmacy or other related health care, it requires a professional degree where the law so provides and meet the requirements of membership, specialisation, licensing and others provided by law";
- the Medical Labour Law, Legislative Decree No. 559, 03/29/1990, which regulates the work of the surgeon on the premises of Public and Private Sector as applicable and Regulations. Article 1 of this rule regulates the work of the Surgeon that has currently enrolled at the Medical College of Peru;
- and the Law of Rural and Urban Marginal Service Health – SERUMS, Law No. 23330, of 12/02/1981 (as earlier described).

Nurses further have to undertake Continuing Professional Development (CPD) to enter management or teaching roles, and they also have to recertify every five years, through regional councils, for which they must demonstrate that they have completed a sufficient amount of CPD's. Universities (which are autonomous) are however under pressure to validate diplomas – which sometimes constitute a quality issue.

The General Directorate of Medicines, Supplies and Drugs (*Dirección General de Medicamentos, Insumos y Drogas*, DIGEMID), which is part of the Ministry of Health, regulates pharmaceuticals, medical devices and other health-related products for all the various health care subsystems in Peru. This responsibility covers regulation of the manufacture, import, export, storage, distribution and commercialisation of these aforementioned products. DIGEMID is also responsible for evaluating products, inspect pharmaceutical establishments and issue certificates and relevant documents. Pharmaceutical establishments should comply with abovementioned practices in order to obtain a registry for their regulated products, that way guaranteeing that pharmaceutical products entering the Peruvian market are safe, effective and of high quality.

DIGEMID interacts with the pharmaceutical industry, at both national and international levels. In addition DIGEMID proposes periodic co-ordination meetings with representatives of different associations, such as ALAFARPE (National Association of Pharmaceutical Laboratories), ADIFAN (Association of National Pharmaceutical Industries), ALAFAL (Latin American Association of Pharmaceutical Laboratories), as well as the unions of Chambers of Commerce (COMSALUD, GUILD HEALTH and COPECOH, Peruvian Guild of Cosmetics and Hygienic Products) involving Pharmaceutical, Medical Devices, Cosmetics and Hygienic products.

DIGEMID furthermore has a key role in pharmacovigilance, access to medication and proper and rational use of medicines. MINSA through DIGEMID in co-ordination with the different entities of health public sector (EsSalud, Health of Armed Forces) establishes a single national list of essential medicines (PNUME). PNUME is updated every two years and covers approximately 80% of the burden of diseases. This list applies across subsystems – and regulates and supervises supply of essential medicines. The constitution moreover prohibits cost regulation of pharmaceuticals (see Chapter 3). DIGEMID's work includes access-centred interventions, notably market analysis to assess whether essential medications are available, and if they are not, the reasons behind the unavailability. DIGEMID thus has a particularly complex role, especially given the challenges of Peru's dually fragmented system, but appears to discharge it extremely well.

The General Directorate of Environmental Health and Food Safety (DIGESA) is responsible for the technical, regulatory, surveillance, survival and control aspects of environmental health, the physical, chemical and biological risk factors external to the person, as well as the food safety of industrially processed food (excepting fishery and aquaculture), and is also the national authority for environmental health and food safety.

DIGESA is responsible for monitoring the safety of products within its jurisdiction, as well as proposing policies related to environmental health and food safety; it also grants and recognises rights through certifications, authorisations, permits and registrations to the products of its competence, carrying out inspections and audits for manufacturing, warehousing and retail. Monitoring is carried out either through routine mechanisms (such as annual monitoring plans), or at request of a party (arising from consumer complaints, for example). DIGESA also provides technical assistance and training to different levels of government regarding their surveillance function. Finally, DIGESA can also declare a state of health emergency in case of inadequate management of solid waste and/or poor quality of water for human consumption.

Discussion regarding reforming DIGESA is underway, given its specialised functions and the scope of its competence. This may, eventually, lead to it becoming an arm's length body, that works closely with MINSA to strengthen public health and prevention in the areas of environmental health and food safety.

Patient involvement and representation in the health system

Some important efforts are made to ensure patient representation in the Peruvian system. The patient rights promotion and protection agency, the independent SUSALUD, is a particularly impressive organisation. Patient rights work undertaken by SUSALUD includes: a patient satisfaction survey, which captures the views of 25 000 patients from across subsystems; in-hospital representation of patients; efforts to improve health literacy among the population, including through increasing user participation. Seven regional patient groups now exist, which are reported as effective at strengthening patient voice; SUSALUD is expected to further decentralise its activities, and is mandated by law to establish 25 regional offices, although this is happening much slower than expected because of a limited budget.

SUSALUD is also involved in dealing with patient complaints, and now has an established complaints management system. The number of patient complaints and positive feedback registered online is increasing, which suggests that users are finding utility in the system. Each hospital in Lima and Ica region also have SUSALUD delegates stationed within the hospital to support patient liaison, and complaint management.

Box 2.8. The role of SUSALUD for patient representation in the health system

The Health Superintendent, SUSALUD, is a particularly important – and effective – actor for health system surveillance. As an independent agency to enforce and protect patient rights, SUSALUD is involved in communication around health system concerns, citizen participation promotion, information dissemination, and pursuing patient complaints. SUSALUD also has two clear and valuable distinctions from other health agencies in Peru: first, SUSALUD is perhaps the only Peruvian health actor with a clear vision for desirous health system transformation; and second, SUSALUD acts for the whole population, regardless of coverage affiliation. SUSALUD's four pillars are UCH; effective coverage (more and better services); patient centeredness and patient rights (protected and enforced by an independent agency); and a 4th pillar striving for stronger, more effective governance from the centre.

Information systems for health performance management

As described in Chatper 1, Peru's Health Information System (HIS) is a software tool that records outpatient activities, and can be processed and consulted by health personnel from MINSA/DIRESA/DISA and their health networks. The HIS is the source of basic information of daily outpatient care recording attendance to health facilities, epidemiological surveillance in terms of morbidity, and preventive and promotional activities. The utility of this information for policy making is limited however, as it is not obtained in a timely manner. Vaccination services, antenatal and child health checks are reported. So too are hospital indicators, including admissions, bed numbers, reasons for admission, and certain activities.

However, to date, the focus of Peru's information infrastructure has been focused on activities, child and maternal health, and infectious diseases. This has been appropriate, given Peru's disease profile, but now needs expanding to cover more non-communicable diseases, in line with the changing epidemiological burden. Additionally, not enough is known about performance – data on patient outcomes is not available, nor is information on costs. Hospitals are understood to record this information, but it is not reported to MINSA. Very few indicators of the quality of health care in Peru exist, which limits the ability to compare variation in performance across subsystems and benchmark Peru's aggregate performance against health systems in other countries.

Connectivity and speed of access to the health information system needs strengthening in order to modernise the information infrastructure. Furthermore, it will be essential for enhancing cost control, as well as monitoring performance of providers and improving quality of health services, that the information systems of the different institutions that make up the fragmented Peruvian health system can be integrated. That way, a more coherent and comprehensive basis for decision making can be created. An in-depth analysis of the Peruvian health information system is the focus of an accompanying publication *OECD Reviews of Health Systems: Monitoring Health System Performance in Peru: Data and Statistics*, (OECD, 2017).

Many Peruvians perceive quality of health care to be poor

In 2015, 72.4% of Peruvians were satisfied with received health care services at a national level, an increase from 70.1% in 2014. Satisfaction with the received services were nevertheless lower in MINSA and EsSalud (72% and 64.9% respectively), while it was higher among the military and police subsector, as well as within the private sector (90.9% and 93.2% respectively) (see Figure 2.8).

Figure 2.8. User satisfaction with received health services, by insurance subsector, 2014 and 2015

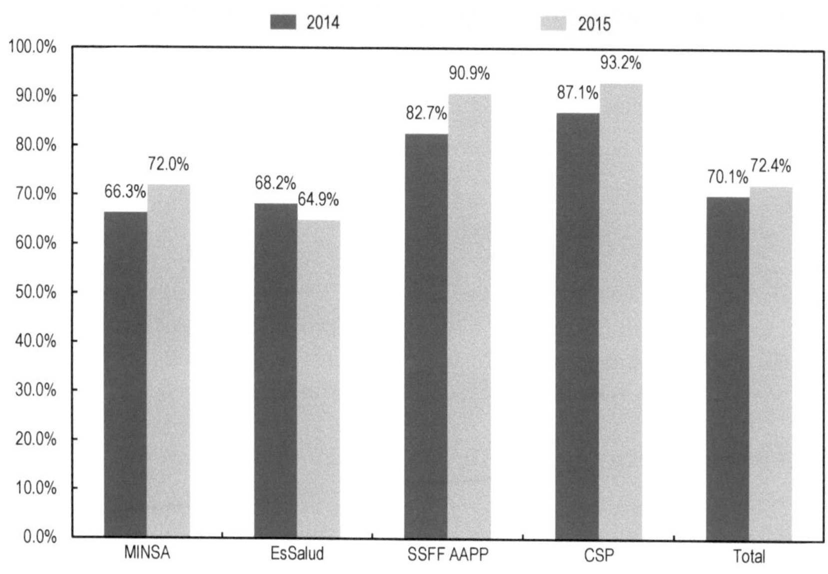

Source: SUSALUD (2016); Instituto Nacional de Estadistica e Informatica – Encuesta Nacional de Satisfaccion de Usuarios en Salud 2015.

Peruvians have nevertheless relatively little confidence in their health-care and medical system, which reflects poorly on the quality of available services (Figure 2.9). Between 2005 and 2010 63% of Colombians, 68% of Mexicans and 73% of Costa Ricans had confidence in their health system. In

Peru this figure only reached 48%, placing Peru behind all chosen benchmark countries.

Figure 2.9. Confidence in health systems in Peru and benchmark countries, 2005-10

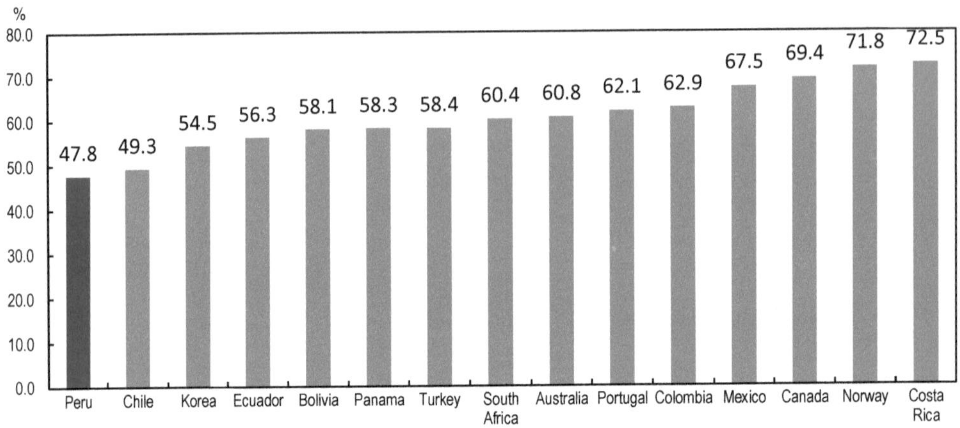

Note: Data for "confidence in health systems" show the percentage of people responding "yes" to the question "Do you have confidence in health care or medical systems?".

Source: Gallup Organisation (2015), Gallup World Monitor (database).

2.4. Improving health care quality in Peru

Quality improvements are needed in the Peruvian health care system. This section highlights some of the key improvement areas and possible strategies that Peru could take in order to enhance the quality of the health care services, thus, leading to better outcomes for the patients.

Peru needs to focus on building quality into UHC strategy

The decentralisation process within the Peruvian health care system is in theory a good measure. Significant powers and competencies within the Peruvian health care system have, however, been decentralised too quickly. Regional autonomy and responsibility is not matched by regional competence. A decentralisation process needs to be backed up with sufficient local capacity, which is arguably not the case for the Peruvian regions. For instance, public health concerns have increased since decentralisation, with vaccination rates falling and some increased incidents of communicable disease outbreaks.

Peru is seeking to strengthen primary care through greater decentralisation. A balance between a return of some core competencies to central authorities, and stronger levers to push regions towards good performance, are however needed. One clear example of an area where core centralised functions seem advisable is around public health, where it seems that a strong health protection and prevention effort needs to be led from the centre, and complemented by local capacity. Moreover, a move towards integrated, networked and multidisciplinary public health teams is advisable. Such teams monitor local health needs and ensures an adequate proactive, preventive approach. Peru may furthermore need to consider ways of compelling regions to fulfil certain functions, for instance ruling that a certain percentage of regional health funds are spent on preventive health activities (as happens in Mexico); again, the centre taking a stronger steering role on the regions' activities.

One area where regions do not have sufficient autonomy is in the co-ordination between SIS and EsSalud, where regions need to refer to Lima to approve co-ordination. This seems an area where regions should be given more capacity, encouragement and support to pursue effective links and co-operation. In order to improve regional capacity and territorial approach, Peru would benefit from further integrating service delivery networks, with a focus on primary care, with funds coming from all subsystems. The before-mentioned *intercambios* (service exchange agreements) is an initiative in this direction and would have to be further developed in order to improve integration of service delivery networks and be an expression of it leading to improved services for the patients. Furthermore, horizontal integration between subsystems can only work if there is more information and transparency on activities, costs etc.

Peru will benefit from the introduction of a national framework on quality and standards

Fragmentation of the system, both regional fragmentation and fragmentation between subsystems, risks undermining the comprehensiveness and efficacy of Peru's quality assurance approaches. Certain key quality assurance functions need to be strengthened, and would likely benefit from being entrusted to a strong, independent, national agency. There is a perception that DIGESA's assurance role has become weaker as a result of reorganisation and decentralisation. Some apparently effective changes have been made in response to this challenge. For instance, DIGESA now engages more in national standard setting and market authorisation for certain chemicals. DIGESA has also introduced a quality accreditation system for target institutions, as well as having begun accrediting local environmental health experts on safety and hygiene, particularly focused on food safety. In particular, DIGESA is monitoring adherence to the ISO international standards regarding the minimum requirements for organisations performing inspections; certifying products, processes and services; as well as certifying of persons.

This approach – the establishment of national standards, and the capacity building at regional or local level to apply them – is a positive development, and one that could be replicated by other agencies as part of a more robust quality assurance function.

Further opportunities for co-operation on quality assurance across subsystems, particularly between SIS and EsSalud, should be sought. EsSalud, for example, has been participating since 2010 in the process of elaboration and updates of PNUME, with other health entities besides DIGEMID such as Health Armed Forces. In addition, DIGEMID is in charge of the Peruvian System of Pharmacovigilance and Technovigilance and it is based on a network of co-ordination and communication in the whole country with the Reference Centers of EsSalud, Health Armed Forces; and regional governments. This should be built upon.

As well as stronger quality assurance agencies, a national focus on quality improvement is needed

As well as strengthening quality assurance, Peru should look to introduce ways to focus attention on quality improvement. Here, lessons can be drawn from OECD countries. Given Peru's highly fragmented health system, a unifying national standards framework for quality could, with sufficient stakeholder buy-in from across the subsystems, have a positive effect on quality improvement. Australia, another highly fragmented health system, is viewed as having taken a successful approach to introducing national quality standards (Box 2.9).

Another way that Peru could move towards quality improvement initiatives applied across the fragmented system would be to introduce voluntary accreditation, initially for hospitals, but also with scope for expansion to other service providers. Such a move would be particularly effective if greater competition could be introduced between subsystems, and if patients could more easily choose between service providers on the basis of public signs of quality. For this to be effective, the *intercambios* would need to be made more operational, or an alternative form of service exchange would need to be found. Nonetheless, Peru should consider introducing a voluntary accreditation model for services, which rewards excellence – in addition to national minimum standards. With this respect, Portugal offers a good model to follow (see Box 2.10).

Box 2.9. National Safety and Quality Health Service Standards in Australia

1. *Governance for Safety and Quality in Health Service Organisations* which describes the quality framework required for health service organisations to implement safe systems.
2. *Partnering with Consumers* which describes the systems and strategies to create a consumer-centred health system by including consumers in the development and design of quality health care.
3. *Prevention and Controlling Healthcare Associated Infections* which describes the systems and strategies to prevent infection of patients within the health care system and to manage infections effectively when they occur to minimise the consequences.
4. *Medication Safety* which describes the systems and strategies to ensure clinicians safely prescribe, dispense and administer appropriate medicines to informed patients.
5. *Patient Identification and Produce Matching* which describes the systems and strategies to identify patients and correctly match their identity with the correct treatment.
6. *Clinical Handover* which describes the systems and strategies for effective clinical communication whenever accountability and responsibility for a patient's care is transferred.
7. *Blood and Blood Products* which describes the systems and strategies for the safe, effective and appropriate management of blood and blood products so the patients receiving blood are safe.
8. *Preventing and Managing Pressure Injuries* which describes the systems and strategies to prevent patients developing pressure injuries and best practice management when pressure injuries occur.
9. *Recognising and Responding to Clinical Deterioration in Acute Health Care* which describes the systems and processes to be implemented by health service organisations to respond effectively to patients when their clinical condition deteriorates.
10. *Preventing Falls and Harm from Falls* which describes the systems and strategies to reduce the incidence of patient falls in health service organisations and best practice management when falls do occur.

Source: OECD (2015), *OECD Reviews of Health Care Quality: Australia 2015: Raising Standards*, OECD Publishing, Paris, http://dx.doi.org/10.1787/9789264233836-en.

Box 2.10. Accreditation of health providers in Portugal

With regards to the number of quality initiatives that have been recently introduced to improve hospital outcome of care, Portugal is ahead of several OECD countries. A number of quality assurance mechanisms have recently been instituted to assure minimum standard of acute care, promote patient safety and encourage hospital benchmarking. Initiatives range from a number of patient safety programmes to the development of sophisticated tools for monitoring and benchmarking hospital outcome of care, as well as a national accreditation system.

The introduction of the national accreditation programme (*Agencia de Calidad Sanitaria de Andalucia*, ACSA) is a key strategy to promote quality in hospital outcome of care. The ACSA programme is the result of a co-operative agreement established between the Ministry of Health of Portugal and the *Consejeria de Salud* of Andaluzia (Spain), with the goal of ensuring co-operation to develop and share a model of health accreditation, while respecting the nature and organisation of each health system. The programme is to some extent based on the Joint Commission International, and recognised as the best fitting the Portuguese context. This way, the programme is intended to meet the key priorities contained in the National Health Programme:

- Patient-centred
- Equitable and sustainable and focuses particularly on clinical management
- Set-up to overcome the major quality issues that have been identified within the national health system

The Portuguese accreditation programme focuses on Services and Health Care Units, Clinical Competencies, Continuous Training Programmes and Health Web Sites. The accreditation process for hospitals (and other health services) is supported by a computer application conceived to support all the phases of this process.

Source: OECD (2015), *OECD Reviews of Health Care Quality: Portugal 2015: Raising Standards*, OECD Publishing, Paris, http://dx.doi.org/10.1787/9789264225985-en.

Peru's data infrastructure needs to focus more on quality and outcomes

There is scope for Peru's data infrastructure to be strengthened, and to be better focused on capturing health system performance, including quality and outcomes data. The health information that is being reported to MINSA seems robust, and in line with Peru's primary health system concerns to date, that is to say a focus on maternal and child health, and public health and infectious diseases. Greater epidemiological scope in reported information is now needed, in particular capturing increasingly prevalent non-communicable diseases.

To establish a core set of information that is published across the whole health system is clearly a significant challenge. Encouragingly, work is ongoing to establish norms and standards that would facilitate interoperability across all subsystems, and would help create a national health data infrastructure. Peru is aiming to have sharable electronic health systems, which can be transferred across all health providers by 2017. A clearly ambitious but commendable goal; OECD and OECD countries has a wealth of knowledge in this domain, and Peru should draw on available expertise and experiences in navigating the political and technical complexities involved.

As well as the obvious challenge that data systematically reported to MINSA and published publicly at present excludes EsSalud and other subsystems, the granularity of reported data could be strengthened. Given the low levels of user's satisfaction with the health system detailed in this chapter, and lack of confidence in the health system from SIS and EsSalud insurees, data reported at the service-provider level could build public confidence in the health system. Data on activities and outcomes at hospital level should be published along with clearly understandable explanation of the information, on a user-friendly platform. A growing majority of OECD countries are now publishing transparent data in this way, at least at the hospital level, and increasingly at the level of other service providers (primary care, ambulatory care), and even by ward or by physician.

Finally, in expanding the health data infrastructure, Peru should look to begin collecting and reporting indicators of health care quality in line with the OECD's internationally comparable definition. Peru should aim to start reporting on OECD's "Health Care Quality Indicator" set (see Table 2.4), and can look to the internationally agreed definitions used to construct the indicators when undertaking their own indicator development work.

Table 2.4. Some of the OECD Health Care Quality Indicators

Indicator	Indicator
Breast cancer survival	Waiting time for femur fracture surgery
Mammography screening	Influenza vaccination for adults over 65
Cervical cancer survival	Smoking rates
Cervical cancer screening	HbA1c testing
Colorectal cancer survival	Poor glucose control
Incidence of vaccine preventable diseases	Retinal exams in diabetics
Coverage for basic vaccination	Amputations in diabetics
AMI 30-day case fatality rate	Diabetes hospital admission
Stroke 30-day case fatality rate	Asthma hospital admission

Source: OECD Health Care Quality Indicators Project – Initial Indicators Report, https://www.oecd.org/els/health-systems/36262514.pdf.

Peru should continue to prioritise patient engagement and education

In the area of patient engagement and education there is much to commend in Peru, and there appears to be longstanding engagement of patient rights groups. The activities of SUSALUD in the few years since establishment have been impressive. SUSALUD's *Junta de Usuarios* in particular seem to be generating effective patient exchange, and should be supported. The Junta de Usarios are SUSALUD representatives, embedded in hospitals, with clearly identified jackets or t-shirts, encouraging patients to exchange their views, concerns and reflections with them. At present, the Junta are established in five priority regions, chosen for both their needs and the feasibility of the scheme, for instance in Arequipa and Cuzco. The Junta de Usuarios's representees are elected, and include representatives from EsSalud, the army and the police forces etc., making them a rare example of cross-system quality scrutiny. The Junta de Usuarios also work closely with pre-existing patient interest groups, of which there are many, for instance there are more than 150 in Lima alone.

There seems to be a good case for investment in the broader roll out of the Junta de Usuarios, for at least three reasons. First, they appear to be an effective way of engaging patient views on the ground, and as part of a national structure, can reflect local perspectives at a national level. Second, given low levels of patient satisfaction and confidence, having identifiable figures in hospitals who can act as liaison and information points seems extremely valuable. And third, as Peru's burden of disease continues to shift towards chronic disease and growing levels of comorbidity – as seen in OECD countries – which demand on-going management, navigation of diverse health providers, and educated and informed patients, the Junta de Usuarios stand to be an extremely valuable resource.

Though there is much to praise in the progress made in terms of improving patient engagement and participation in Peru, there are still areas where Peru could learn from OECD countries. In OECD countries patient groups have been formulating increasingly sophisticated understandings of patient needs, and lobbying for change in a system-wide way, with focus including appropriate models of care, or financial access. The experience of Denmark is one from which Peru, and Peru's relatively young Junta de Usuarios, could learn (see Box 2.11).

Box 2.11. Improving patient safety in Denmark

The lead organisation for improving the safety of health care in Denmark is the *Danish Society for Patient Safety*. It is a third-sector (non-profit) organisation made up of health care professionals, patient and research organisations, the pharmaceutical and medical device industry, hospitals and local government. As well as producing tools (such as a Root Cause Analysis Tool Kit) and guidance (such as on how better hospital design can improve safety), it also engages in campaigns and advocacy. Its *Danish Safer Hospital Programme* aims to achieve a 15% reduction in mortality and 30% reduction in harm by reducing the number of cardiac arrests, eliminating hospital infections, reducing pressure ulcers and preventing medication errors and other actions.

A distinctive feature of the Society is its emphasis on patients and carers as key partners in improving health care safety. A number of tools and campaigns have been developed to support this. Amongst the most well-known is the Society's *Patient Handbook*, designed to accompany a hospital admission. The Handbook covers a range of topics, much of which is distilled into the following ten Safety Tips for Patients:

1. Speak up if you have any questions or concerns
2. Let us know about your habits
3. Take notes during your stay
4. More ears listen better
5. You can let somebody else handle your consultation
6. Check your personal data
7. Ask about your operation
8. Tell us if it hurts
9. Before discharge from hospital
10. Know the medication you are taking

Another patient-oriented initiative is called *Hello Healthcare*. This recognises that there are significant barriers for patients to overcome when dealing with the health care system, such as the power gap between doctor and patient or lack of staff time, which pose safety risks. The campaign encourages patients to participate more actively in their health care, and expect to be heard and listened to.

Source: http://www.patientsikkerhed.dk/.

Conclusions

Health system coverage in Peru has increased rapidly during the last decades. However, in order to achieve effective UHC it is now essential not only to prioritise provide coverage for the whole population, but also to ensure that it leads to accessible and high quality health care services for all. A long term strategy for UHC and a target for when it should be achieved is advisable for Peru in order to bring all relevant actors together in a common agenda. This strategy would have to involve ways of guaranteeing health insurance to non-poor self-employed and informal workers by expanding the scope of SIS. A national framework to meet the health needs of remote and rural populations is another important step Peru could take to set standards that all regions must meet in terms of basic health service provision.

One of the biggest challenges for Peru in terms of health care quality is how to deal with the highly fragmented health care system. Clear definitions of the national and regional governments' roles will need to be established in order to improve efficiency and sustainability. Key quality assurance functions would also need to be strengthened and Peru should therefore develop and introduce a national framework on quality and standards. In order to make a more efficient use of the supply of care, Peru would benefit from further integrating service delivery networks (promoting the so called *intercambios*), with a focus on primary care.

Furthermore, Peru could gain from re-centralising basic health promotion and disease prevention activities, moving towards integrated, networked and multidisciplinary public health teams. Merging health information data from different subsystems and making recording and reporting of health information obligatory for health providers, would also allow a more comprehensive picture about health care system performance and thus lead to a more solid base for benchmarking and further decision making for quality improvement.

An increase in, and more even distribution of, human resources for health is needed, specifically in terms of staffing in rural and remote areas is specifically important. A range of potential strategies for Peru to pursue in this regard this have been presented in this chapter. Promoting the use of innovative health service delivery to provide adequate level of access with fewer physicians (e.g. through telemedicine) is also an option to deliver health services for difficult-to-reach populations.

References

El Comercio (2015a), "Presupuesto del SIS requiere aumentar en 240% en cinco años", El Comercio, 28/05/2015, retrieved from http://elcomercio.pe/economia/peru/presupuesto-sis-requiere-crecer-240-cinco-anos-noticia-1814458.

El Comercio (2015b), "Salud en el Perú: acuerdan meta de 170 hospitales estratégicos", El Comercio, retrieved from http://elcomercio.pe/peru/pais/salud-peru-acuerdan-meta-170-hospitales-estrategicos-noticia-1818575.

FIIAPP – Fundación Internacional e Iberoamericana (2015), "Peru Visits Colombia to Learn About its Health Equity Monitoring System", http://www.fiiapp.org/en/noticias/peru-visits-colombia-learn-health-equity-monitoring-system/.

IADB – Inter-American Development Bank (2015), "Perú: Programa de Modernización de la Gestión para la Cobertura Universal de Salud: (PE-L1169) Propuesta para el Desarrollo de la Operación", BID, Lima.

INEI – Instituto Nacional de Estadísticañ e Informática (2016), *Condiciones de Vida en el Perú*, retrieved from Lima: https://www.inei.gob.pe/media/MenuRecursivo/boletines/informe-tecnico-n02_condiciones-vida_octnovdic15.pdf.

Jiménez, M. et al. (2015), "Analysis of the Health Care Labor Market in Peru", International Bank for Reconstruction and Development / The World Bank.

Knaul, F. et al. (2011), "Household Catastrophic Health Expenditures: A Comparative Analysis of Twelve Latin American and Caribbean Countries", *Salud Pública de México*, Vol. 53, Suplemento 2, pp. 85-95, http://www.scielosp.org/pdf/spm/v53s2/05.pdf.

Madueño, M., J. Alarcón and C. Sanabria (2003), "Análisis de la brecha entre oferta y demanda de servicios de salud para la programación de la inversión sectorial de mediano plazo", PHRPlus, No. 272.

MEF – Ministerio de Economía y Finanzas (2015), "¿Qué es Presupuesto por Resultados (PpR)?", retrieved from http://www.mef.gob.pe/index.php?option=com_content&view=article&id=2122&.

MINSA – Ministerio de Salud (2015a), "Cuentas nacionales de salud Perú 1995-2012", retrieved from http://bvs.minsa.gob.pe/local/MINSA/3248.pdf.

MINSA (2015b), "Información de Recursos Humanos en el Sector Salud: Perú 2014", retrieved from http://observatorio.inforhus.gob.pe/publicaciones/bibliograficos/libro21/polifoliar_2014.pdf.

MINSA (2011), "Programa nacional de formación en salud familiar y comunitaria", Dirección General de Gestión del Desarrollo de Recursos Humanos, Dirección de Gestión de Capacidades en Salud, Lima.

OECD (2017), *Monitoring Health System Performance in Peru: Data and Statistics,* OECD Publishing, Paris, http://dx.doi.org/10.1787/9789264282988-en.

OECD (2016a), "OECD Health Statistics 2016", OECD Publishing, Paris, http://dx.doi.org/10.1787/health-data-en.

OECD (2016b), *OECD Reviews of Health Systems: Mexico 2016*, OECD Publishing, Paris, http://dx.doi.org/10.1787/9789264230491-en.

OECD (2016c), *Health Workforce Policies in OECD Countries: Right Jobs, Right Skills, Right Places*, OECD Health Policy Studies, OECD Publishing, Paris, http://dx.doi.org/10.1787/9789264239517-en.

OECD (2015a), *Multi-dimensional Review of Peru: Volume 1. Initial Assessment*, OECD Publishing, Paris, http://dx.doi.org/10.1787/9789264243279-en.

OECD (2015b), *Health at a Glance 2015: OECD Indicators*, OECD Publishing, Paris, http://dx.doi.org/10.1787/health_glance-2015-en.

OECD (2015c), *OECD Reviews of Health Systems: Colombia 2016*, OECD Publishing, Paris, http://dx.doi.org/10.1787/9789264248908-en.

Pan American Health Organisation (2012), *Health in the Americas*, 2012 Edition: Country Volume.

Seinfeld, J. and N. Besich (2014), *Universal Health Coverage Assessment: Peru*, Global Network for Health Equity (GNHE).

Seinfeld, J., V. Montañez and N. Besich (2013), *The Health Insurance System in Peru: Towards a Universal Health* Insurance, Global Development Network: Strengthening Institutions to Improve Public Expenditure Accountability.

SUSALUD – Superintendencia Nacional de Salud (2016), "El Sistema de Salud: Evolucion y Aspectos Claves", Presentacion para la OCDE.

Vermeersch, C., A. Medici and R. Narvarez (2014), *Universal Health Coverage for Inclusive and Sustainable Development: Country Summary Report for Peru*, Health, Nutrition and Population Global Practice, World Bank Report, September.

World Bank (2016), "World Development Indicators", retrieved from http://databank.worldbank.org/data/reports.aspx?source=world-development-indicators.

Chapter 3

Sustainability and efficiency of Peru's government-funded health system

Peru has made substantial progress toward universal health coverage, increasing population health insurance coverage from 37% in 2004 to 83%, according to latest estimates from SUSALUD. The Sistema Integral de Salud (SIS), provided by government, has been the main source of this expanded coverage. Despite such progress, however, much remains to be done.

This chapter identifies the key challenges that the government-funded health insurance system, namely SIS, must face in the future. An efficient and sustainable health insurance scheme should: i) ensure effective and financial access to health services, ii) use resources efficiently through strategic purchasing; iii) generate sufficient and sustainable resources; and, iv) manage population health risk and institutional financial risk.

Peru needs to move forward in all these areas if it wants to set the conditions for an efficient and sustainable publicly-funded health insurance system.

Introduction

Peru's explicit policy goal to reach universal health coverage (UHC) by 2021 means getting more out of the available resources, especially given the moderate outlook for economic growth in the coming years. According to the International Monetary Fund (IMF), Peru's average real GDP growth is projected to be between 3.5 and 3.9% between 2017 and 2022, compared to around 5% for emerging markets and developing economies more broadly. This means that limited resources (financial, personnel, infrastructure, inputs) have to be put to best possible use. Exploiting efficiency gains will also be crucial to meet rapidly growing health care demand.

This chapter presents an analysis of sustainability and efficiency as two components health system performance. Two types of sustainability are considered, in Section 3.1. Political sustainability – which refers to the continuity and commitment of policies and strategies by key actors; and, financial sustainability – which refers to the adequacy resource flows to guarantee the continuity of the expected outcomes of the policy (Mokate, 2001). The analysis of efficiency, in Section 3.2, examines how well available resources are being used. In both sections, the focus is on the government-funded sector of the Peruvian health system, that is, the *Seguro Integral de Salud* (SIS).

Sustainability is linked to efficiency. Inefficiencies put the financial sustainability of the system at risk, while political instability can also lead to inefficiency, if governments close programmes implemented in a different administration, for example, or use programmes for political gain. Hence, recommendations for improving the sustainability and efficiency of SIS are considered together in Section 3.3.

3.1. Financial and political sustainability in the government-funded health system

One high-level benchmark of health system efficiency is international comparison of life expectancy at birth and total health care spending. If these are indicators are arranged in a scatter plot, for all countries in LAC and the OECD, Peru lies above the regression line in both 1995 and 2013. This suggests that Peru is relatively efficient at converting health expenditure into longer life expectancy. This is consistent with other basic health indicators. As discussed in Chapter 1, for example, Peru has achieved the Millennium Development Goal (MDG) # 4 of reducing infant and under-5 mortality rates by two thirds in 2008 and 2006, respectively. In the case of MDG 5, reducing by three quarters the maternal mortality ratio, Peru was able to reduce to 68 but did not reach its goal of 63 deaths per 100 000 live births. Nevertheless, these achievements should be praised.

To get a more thorough view of Peru's health sector efficiency, however, other dimensions of efficiency should be examined. It would be useful, for example, to know the extent to which resources are wasted through imbalances in inputs and activities, such as avoidable hospital admissions. Unfortunately, very few comparative data is available for Peru on such measures. This in itself suggests that one of the key challenges facing Peru concerns limited information systems, as outlined further detail in the companion publication *Monitoring Health System Performance in Peru: Data and Statistics* (OECD, 2017).

A substantial share of the Peruvian population remains without formal health insurance

As explained in Chapter 1, the signing of the National Agreement (or *Acuerdo Nacional*, AN) in 2002 was a key milestone on Peru's path to universal health coverage. A key weakness of the AN, however, is that it does not provide a clear picture of the architecture of universal health coverage in the long run. The AN specifies broad goals (namely, achievement of UHC), but does not include a technical discussion of how the health system should be configured to provide it. It does not specify, for example, whether the various subsystems within the current configuration will be maintained and, if so, how to reach a more equitable and efficient distribution of resources across them and across geographic regions. Neither does the AN specify how to affiliate the persistently large informal sector in a health system that relies heavily on formal sector contributions tied to formal labour contracts on the one hand, and general taxes on the other.

The lack of a clear vision for the future health system poses a challenge to its political and financial sustainability. Individual initiatives may fall within the strategic framework envisioned by the AN, for example, but typically do not consider the system as a whole. They fail to contribute, therefore, to an overall approach on moving towards universal health coverage. The most important example concerns SIS. Although the creation of SIS was the key driver to increase health insurance coverage, the long-run plan for SIS is still unclear in terms of its role in reaching the remaining 17% the population without health insurance.

To reach universal health insurance coverage, Peru needs to find ways to cover those who remain without insurance. Most individuals in this group are informal or self-employed workers. A critical challenge is that a substantial number, however, are less poor than those currently affiliated by SIS, but poorer than those covered by EsSalud, meaning that they fall between two stools. In 2014, "non-poor" individuals constituted the vast majority of the uninsured, as shown in Table 3.1.

Table 3.1. Total household expenditure per capita and population covered by type of insurance and poverty status, 2014

	Extreme poor	Poor	Non poor	Subtotal
Uninsured	1,331.75	2,894.93	7,690.83	6,784.25
	0.80%	4.80%	25.50%	31.10%
Only EsSalud	1,424.95	3,316.85	9,706.77	9,262.18
	0.00%	1.70%	22.80%	24.50%
Only private	0	3,898.18	18,449.99	18,366.63
	0.00%	0.00%	0.90%	0.90%
Only SIS	1,346.24	2,567.01	5,622.21	4,320.37
	3.40%	11.90%	23.70%	39.00%
Only other type	1,367.49	3,453.92	12,305.31	12,050.99
	0.00%	0.10%	2.40%	2.50%
More than one	927.07	2,905.01	18,278.24	18,185.08
	0.00%	0.00%	2.00%	2.00%
Total	**1,343.97**	**2,723.75**	**8,194.25**	**6,896.72**
	4.30%	**18.40%**	**77.40%**	**100.00%**

Source: Authors based on ENAHO 2014.

Initiatives to encourage uninsured groups to affiliate to SIS have had limited success

SIS has experimented with different voluntary schemes to expand its coverage to the uninsured non-poor population. In 2007, SIS created the "semi-contributory" regime for people with a limited ability to pay.[1] In 2008, access was given to microenterprises' workers in the semi-contributory regime with payments made by the employer and matched by the MEF. In 2009, the AUS Law adopted the so-called semi-contributory regime.

Most recently, in 2013, a new attempt to include non-poor population was made through SIS Entrepreneurs, which affiliated independent workers who voluntarily signed up for the New Unique Simplified Regime (*Nuevo Régimen Único Simplificado*, NRUS) of the National Superintendence of Customs and Tax Administration (*Superintendencia Nacional de Aduanas y Administración Tributaria*, SUNAT). This tax regime was created as an incentive for independent workers to file taxes, and hence increase the tax base. Affiliation to SIS is automatic through this mechanism, since SUNAT provides the list to SIS of the population enrolled. No additional payments are required besides paying taxes. The key incentive is that the NRUS is a much simpler tax filing system than the regular one.

These attempts have been largely unsuccessful, however, and semi-contributory affiliation remains small. In December 2015, only 1.3% of all SIS beneficiaries were in the semi-contributory regime (SIS, 2016).

A technical roadmap towards fully achieving UHC is not in place

It is clear, then, that Peru has struggled to extend formal health insurance to those belonging to the non-poor and informal sectors. The challenge is to design effective incentives to encourage, or require, the uninsured population to affiliate with SIS or EsSalud. Lack of affiliation translates into the inefficient alternative of out-of-pocket expenditures and, of course, difficulty in fully achieving UHC.

Peru does not have, however, a clear road-map in place to guide further progress toward fully achieving UHC. A national strategy that details roles and objectives for SIS, as well as EsSalud and other insurers, is necessary given the currently highly fragmented health system with very unequal distribution of resources, both geographically and across subsystems.

Some fundamental questions that must be answered to fully realise UHC include: will funds be pooled across SIS and EsSalud in the long run? Or will new resources be mobilised to make allocations between those publicly insured by SIS more equal to those available in EsSalud? Will health services belonging to the different subsystems be made available to all, irrespective of the health insurance, to assure a more equitable system? And if so, how?

Current levels of funding mean that SIS will struggle to enrol more individuals

According to the Pan-American Health Organisation, a minimum of 6% GDP committed to public spending on health systems is required to provide an essential package of services (Organización Panamericana de la Salud, 2007). Similarly, Xu et al. (2010) conclude that a 5-6% GDP spent on publicly-funded health services would considerably reduce the incidence of financial catastrophe amongst households and individuals.

Peru committed to raising public health expenditure (PHE) to 6% of GDP in 2007 but still falls considerably short of this figure. Figure 3.1 shows PHE as percentage of GDP for LAC and OECD countries. Peru's PHE is very low in comparison to the LAC average, and even compared to LAC countries with lower GDP per capita. From a standpoint of meeting the UHC goal of financial protection, Xu et al. (2010) suggested out-of-pocket (OOP) expenditure should not exceed 15-20% of THE for the system to provide financial protection. As discussed in Chapter 1, OOP in Peru represented 29% of total health expenditure, a figure significantly above the OECD average, although similar to other LAC countries.

Figure 3.1. Public health expenditure as percentage of GDP, Latin America and OECD, 2013

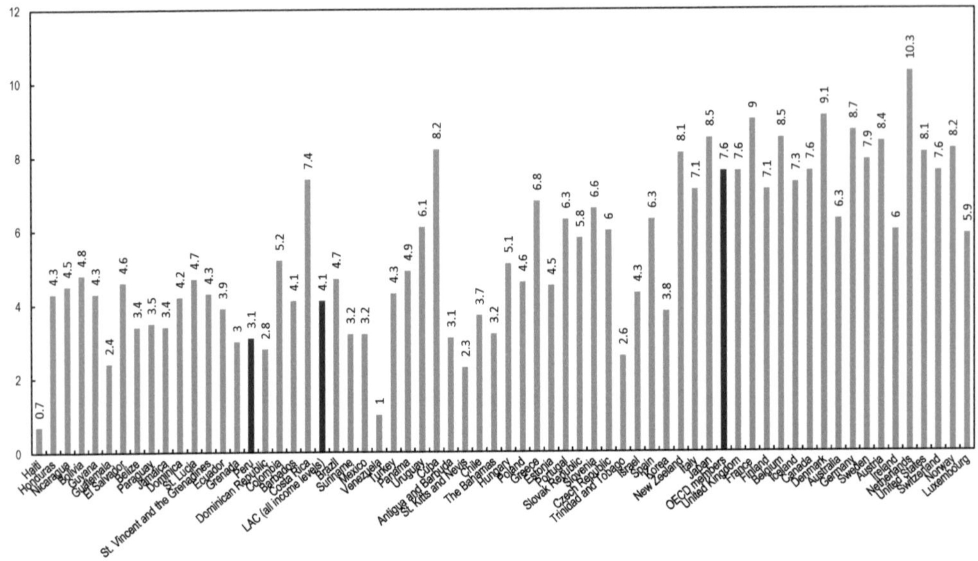

Note: Countries are organised from left to right by ascending GDP per capita (measured in international dollars, adjusted by purchasing power parity, PPP).

Source: World Bank (2016), "World Development Indicators", retrieved from http://databank.worldbank.org/data/reports.aspx?source=world-development-indicators.

It must be noted that Peru's commitment has increased over time: from USD 148 to USD 368 PHE per capita (measured in constant 2011 international dollars adjusted by PPP) between 2000 and 2013. Nevertheless, low PHE is one of the key challenges of the Peruvian health system that has been repeatedly highlighted by former reviews (Francke, 2013).

SIS is generally under-funded, even for its current service obligations

Contrary to other mandatory health insurance systems in the region (such as Colombia or Uruguay), SIS does not collect its own funds. Instead, SIS negotiates with MEF on a yearly basis for its funding allocation. But this does not mean that SIS, in practice, can rely on resources that are consistent with the number of its affiliates or the actuarial cost of providing benefits. In 2011, the Law of Public Financing of the Subsidised and Semi-Contributory Regimes established that SIS would receive funding based on the premium and the number of beneficiaries. However, this rule is not binding and has never been implemented in practice.[2]

An actuarial study, presented in 2015 using 2012 data (SIS, 2015b), established an average expected cost of S/.360 per affiliate per year (equivalent to USD 136 or EUR 106). In 2015, SIS's average expenditure per affiliate was S/.82.81 (including all regimes) (equivalent to USD 31 or EUR 24), which represents a mere 23% of the estimated cost. Similar gaps between the expected cost and actual allocations to SIS have been identified almost since the inception of SIS (Prieto et al., 2014). Figure 3.2 shows SIS's final annual budget per affiliate and average funding ("transfer") per beneficiary.[3] Between 2009 and 2015, SIS's total budget grew on average 21% in nominal terms. Funding per beneficiary grew on average 11.5%, but this still does not match the actuarial cost of the benefits package. Furthermore, the increase in the average amount SIS receives per beneficiary has not been the result of an estimated change in the actuarial cost of providing the benefits packages, but rather the result of separate results-based financing schemes managed by MEF (see more on this below).

Figure 3.2. SIS's annual budgets and transfers per beneficiaries, 2002-16

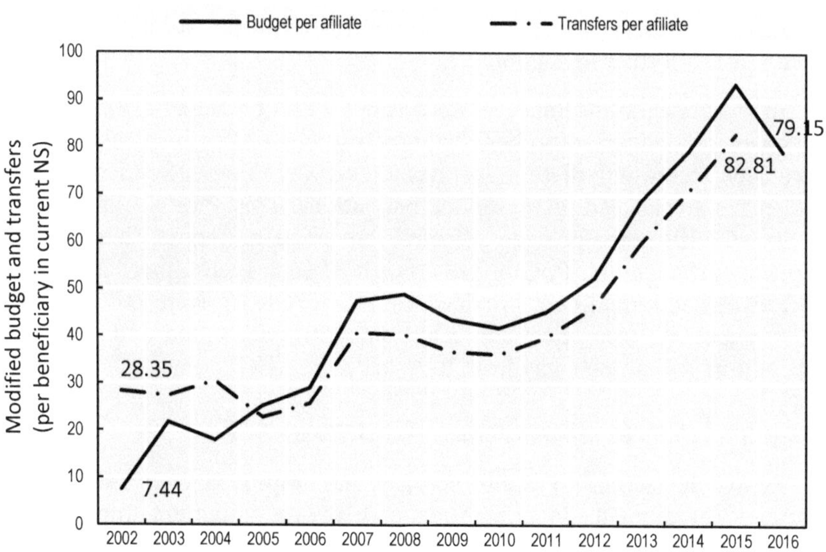

Note: Beneficiaries in 2016 consider data until January 2016.

Source: Based on SIS (2015), "Boletín Estadístico Seguro Integral de Salud", SIS.

Taking advantage of the lack of a clear financing formula for SIS, MEF was able to decrease SIS's budget by as much as 5.6% in the public sector budget for 2016. The decision to reduce SIS's budget was made after considering the reduction in GDP growth, with little consideration for the cost of providing insurance coverage for more than 16 million Peruvians, and without any explicit decision on a reduction of the scope of the benefits plan or the number of people covered by SIS. As a result, SIS announced that 500 000 subsidised affiliates would be "transferred" to the semi-contributory regime, and required to pay for their affiliation. This "forced" transfer across regimes seems to be the consequence of budget restrictions, rather than the result of a thought-through policy to help those able to move to the semi-contributory scheme. It is unclear whether this half a million people will be able to transfer to the semi-contributory regime, or will simply join the uninsured. The later would represent a backward step away from universal coverage.

Similarly, several recent reforms have created significant challenges for the financial sustainability of EsSalud. These include allowing EsSalud beneficiaries to affiliate to a private insurer for low-cost services; reducing EsSalud's income as part of the anti-crisis plan in 2009; and establishing different levels of contribution for public sector workers (those with higher salaries now making less than the standard 9% contribution). These issues are discussed further in Section 1.4.

In short, health insurance in Peru is not based on actuarial estimates of the coverage obligations to beneficiaries. Although SIS' financial resources have been increasing, there is still has a long way to go before it receives a budget better-matched to its service obligations. This severely limits SIS's ability to efficiently provide effective coverage and risks financial and political sustainability. Possibly as a result of such issues, there has been a shift away for formal care provided by SIS towards private providers and self-medication (see Section 2.1), implying increased out-of-pocket expenditure and a step away from fully realising UHC.

Large shortfalls in infrastructure characterise SIS

Peruvians' access to health services has improved over recent years thanks to investments in infrastructure. However important infrastructure gaps within SIS and the wider Peruvian health system still remain. According to one estimate from Bambarén and Alatrista (2015), the infrastructure investment gap for primary health care is estimated at USD 478 million, equivalent to 101 new health centres, 180 new basic health units, and 5 new basic hospitals. Peru has also important gaps in terms of the number of hospital beds when compared to other countries in the region and the OECD. As shown in Figure 1.18, Peru has 1.5[4] beds per

1 000 population while Argentina, Chile and Brazil have 4.7, 2.3 and 2.1, respectively. These estimates, however, do not consider variables such as differences in need due to the epidemiological transition, or expansion of health insurance coverage.

To respond to such shortfalls in infrastructure, MINSA has improved the response capacity of 748 health facilities – called "strategic facilities" – to strengthen primary health care. Additionally, MINSA reached an agreement with regional governments in 2015 to strengthen 170 provincial strategic hospitals, 22 regional hospitals and 12 national hospitals by 2021. The implementation of these investments has been slow, however, due to complex public sector investment processes.

These are important steps, but could be more effective if a more coherent vision of the entire system was brought into view. The estimates associated with the strategic facilities do not consider, for example, the availability of infrastructure from other sectors (such as private physicians' offices). By looking at the health sector infrastructure as a whole (as opposed to focusing on the public sector only) investment plans could be designed more sustainably and efficiently.

Workforce shortages are also a particular challenge

WHO (2006) estimated that countries with fewer than 25 physicians, nurses and midwives per 10 000 population generally fail to achieve adequate coverage rates for health care interventions prioritised by the Millennium Development Goals (MDG). Similarly, the 2005 Toronto meeting established a minimum density of 10 physicians per 10 000 population (PAHO, 2005). In addition to the access problem implied by shortfalls in workforce, inefficiencies may also emerge as a result of inadequate level, mix or distribution of human resources.

In 2009, Peru had a national average of 9.4 physicians and 19.5 physicians, nurses and midwives per 10 000 population (MINSA/DGGRHS, 2013 Análisis de Situación de Salud). By 2013 this had increased to 17 physicians and 22 nurses per 10 000 population, indicating that Peru has reached the minimum at national-level. Differences in the distribution across geographic regions, however, remain. Figure 3.3 shows that only 10 of the 25 departments have the minimum number of physicians (according to WHO minimum standards). More promisingly, the ratio of nurses per physicians rose to 1.1 in 2012, which is above the goal of reaching a 1.0 ratio (MINSA/DGGRHS, 2013).

Figure 3.3. Health human resources density per 10 000 population by department, 2014

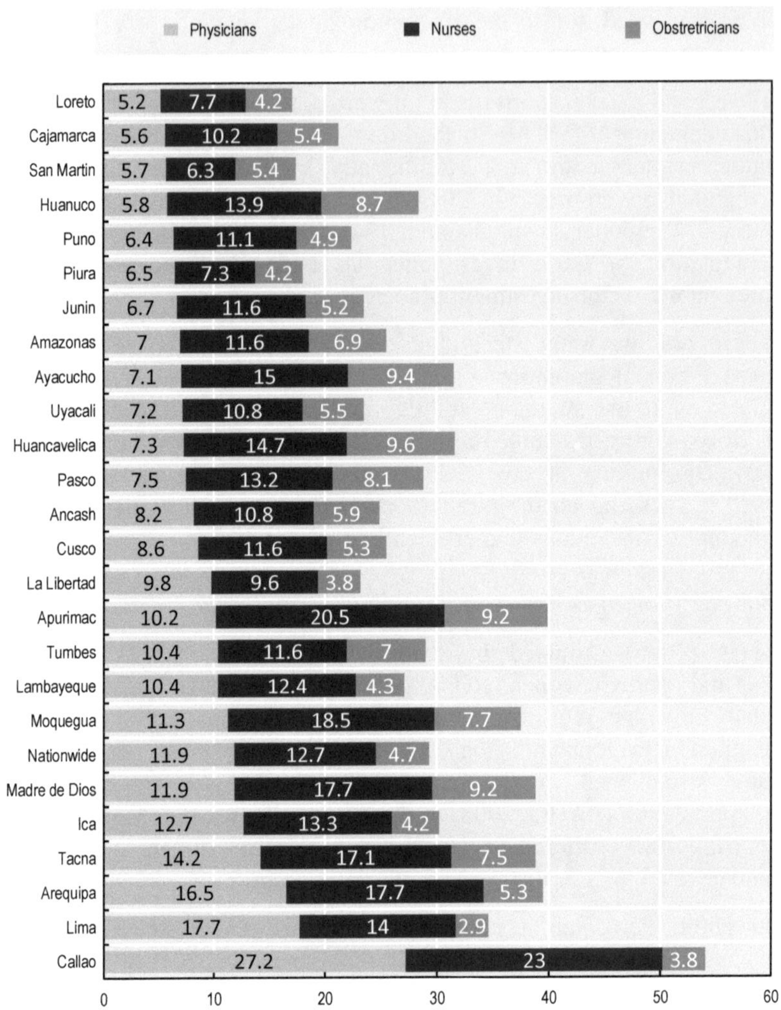

Source: MINSA (2015), "Información de Recursos Humanos en el Sector Salud: Perú 2014", retrieved from http://observatorio.inforhus.gob.pe/publicaciones/bibliograficos/libro21/polifoliar_2014.pdf.

Peru has taken several important steps to tackle health care work force challenges (Table 3.2). First, a National Health Personnel Register called INFORHUS was created, in 2013. INFORHUS' main goal is to monitor the regional availability of human resources in order to adequately plan for current and future needs. Second, a National Training Programme in Family and Community Health (PROFAM) was adopted in 2009, implemented through universities. It has the goal of strengthening primary care through an increase in the availability of basic health care teams (*Equipos Básicos de Salud* – EBS). PROFAM also has the potential to improve efficiency, through better integrating the health system with strong primary care at the centre. A third policy was the strengthening of decentralised management of human resources by strengthening regional decision-making (MINSA/DGGRHS, 2013). The goal was to improve regional management of human resources and give the subnational level the tools to improve the distribution of health care workers, based on local needs. Finally, in 2013, MINSA established a human resource management policy to advance the reform of wages and regulations in the health care sector, including financial incentives to encourage better productivity and geographic distribution (one of the key problems in the distribution was the lack of incentives to maintain staff in more remote areas). The 2013 policy increased wages for human resources in these areas and offered more job stability.

Table 3.2. Human resources policies implemented and the problem or challenge addressed

Policy	Problem or challenge addressed
INFORHUS: health human resources information system	Lack of information on geographical distribution of health workers, which challenges human resources planning
PROFAM: Training of primary care teams	Expansion of primary care model
Regional HR management training	Lack of technical capacity in the regions to plan for the local need of health workers
Health HR payment policy	Provide incentives to improve performance and geographical distribution of HR

Source: Authors.

The key challenge going forward will be to fully exploit each of these policies as step towards achieving a more equal and integrated health care system. Planning must consider the health networks across sectors and regions, and not be limited to the public network. If the analysis of human resources gaps does not take into account those in the private sector, for example, there will be the possibility of wasted investment or persisting inequity.

… yet pressure to add further services to the SIS benefit package is growing

SIS's basic benefits package, PEAS (*Plan Esencial de Aseguramiento de Salud*), was first defined in 2009. It covers 140 health conditions, representing approximately 65% of Peru's burden of disease. Some, albeit rudimentary, evidence was used to design the benefits package (Prieto et al.,

2014). Although current regulations state that the package should be updated every two years; this has never been done in practice, and no institutionalised processes has been put in place to do so. The lack of a systematic, evidence-based updating processes is likely to challenge the legitimacy and political sustainability of PEAS in the longer term (Glassman et al., 2016).

To respond to evolving health care needs, Peru introduced two additional plans in 2010, the "Complementary Plan" and the "Exceptional Coverage Plan". These, however, represent additions to PEAS rather than a systematic and planned revision of the benefit package (see Table 3.2). Services included within the Complementary Plan do not require any approval by SIS, but are subject to a cap on spending. Services included within the Exceptional Coverage Plan do require a case-by-case approval but are not, in theory, subject to a spending limit. Put together, PEAS, the Complementary Plan and the Exceptional Coverage Plan are intended to include all possible services, with the exception of those explicitly excluded by PEAS.

An additional element is the Hope Plan, which covers five cancers, renal failure, and some rare and orphan diseases. Although the list of rare and orphan diseases includes 399 diseases, only eight are included in the Hope Plan, leaving the remaining 391 without guaranteed coverage. For the cancers and renal failure, all levels of services are covered from promotional, preventive, curative, to palliative care for terminal patients (PEAS covers diagnostic services). These services are funded through the Intangible Solidary Fund for Health (*Fondo Intangible Solidario de Salud*, FISSAL). FISSAL was originally a complementary financing source set up in 2002, financed through donations and therefore initially functioning as a private fund. In 2011, it was transformed into a public fund operating under SIS with the objective of financing care for some high cost diseases. These somewhat fragmented arrangements are summarised in Table 3.3 and Figure 3.4.

Figure 3.4 presents service and financial coverage of the explicit health plans in a figure. The horizontal axis represents service coverage, from more frequent and less complex services, to less frequent and more complex. The vertical axis represents the financial coverage in terms of percentage of the cost being covered of a given service. Spending on most conditions within PEAS is moderated by a financial cap, although caps are not binding for less expensive services. Financial coverage is 100% for these less expensive services. For other services, effective financial coverage drops, represented by the sloping section of PEAS coverage.

Table 3.3. Summary of health plans

	PEAS	Complementary Plan[a]		Hope Plan[b]
Date approved	Nov 2009	Dec 2012		Nov 2012
Coverage	140 health condition (approx.65% of BOD) with financial caps.	Does not require approval: All health conditions and health services considered in PEAS with a financial cap are covered with a new financial cap. All health conditions and health services not considered in PEAS, and not explicitly excluded, with a financial cap.	Requires approval: Provides financial coverage above the existing financial caps. Coverage provided on a case by case approval.	Five types of cancers, leukaemia, lymphomas, chronic renal failure, and rare and orphan diseases (only the 8 considered very high priority)
Financing agent	SIS, EsSalud and some insurers	SIS		SIS & FISSAL
Target population	Beneficiaries of SIS, EsSalud and some insurers	SIS: Subsidised and semi-contributory regimes		SIS: Subsidised regime
Selection criteria	Based on BOD, frequency and some cost-effectiveness	Not explicit. Meant to ensure that the scope of coverage was not reduced by the introduction of PEAS.		Frequency.
Updates	None	Financial cap was increased in 2011. Two previous plan were merged into one in 2012.		Rare and orphan diseases were included in 2014.

a) In October 2010, two plans were approved through SIS' Resolutions: RJ No. 133-2010/SIS and RJ No. 134-2010/SIS. The first defined the Complementary Plan and the second the Extraordinary Coverage. These plans and their coverages were later included as the Complementary Plan (using the same name as before) with the two types of coverages described above.

b) In April 2012, the List of high cost diseases was approved through MINSA's Resolution No. 325-2012/MINSA. This list was later included as part of the Hope Plan in November 2012.

Source: Authors.

Figure 3.4. Service and financial coverage of health plans

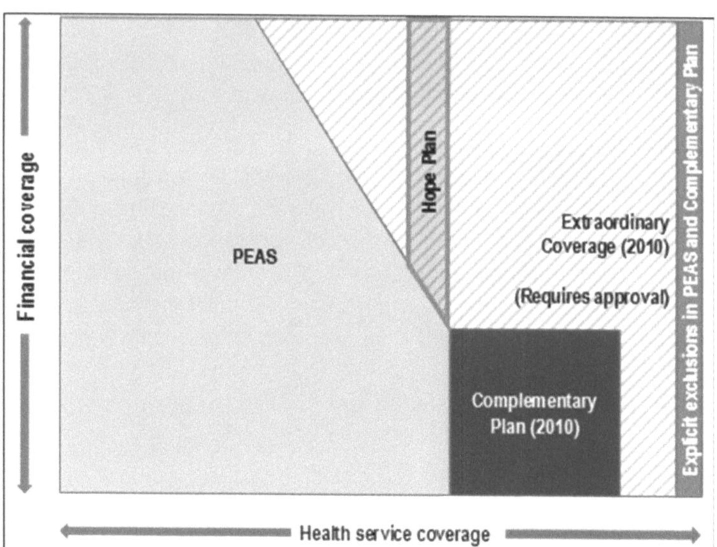

As the former description illustrates, Peru's ensemble of health insurance plans constitute a highly fragmented approach to services covered and financial protection offered. SIS and FISSAL, for example, offer the same service coverage for some health problems. PEAS covers diagnostic services for uterine cancer, for example, as does the Hope Plan, and there is no mechanism to determine which insurer finances these overlapping services. Results-based budgeting programmes, explored further in Section 3.2, complicate the funding picture still further. There is, overall, a substantial need for more systematic and evidence based processes to inform the coverage decisions for the various benefits packages and, ideally, consolidate them into a single pool.

Expansion of benefit packages without actuarial analysis risks the political and financial sustainability of SIS

As discussed, an important challenge to the sustainability of SIS is the way benefits packages and the beneficiary population groups have been expanded. Although expansions of SIS's benefits basket are important steps toward fully realising UHC, they have not always been underpinned by sound estimates of the costs implied. The list of high-cost diseases covered by FISSAL, for example, was determined largely by prevalence estimates, without accompanying cost-effectiveness and budget-impact analyses.

Expansion of benefit packages without the necessary cost-effectiveness and budget-impact analysis limits SIS's ability to manage its service obligations. Ideally, decisions to increase population coverage should be accompanied by actuarial analysis of the capacity of the public network to provide the additional services. If not, such changes to liabilities constitute shocks to the political and financial sustainability of SIS.

From the patient's point of view, SIS is accountable to the problems that may arise with access, for example, or quality. Who defines or expands coverage, and whether or not it is fully financed, is arguably not relevant for SIS beneficiaries. Service users care most about access and quality, rather than underlying financing mechanisms. Therefore, the sustainability and legitimacy of SIS is put at risk when expansions are carried out without a more considered approach, ideally with public and patient involvement.

3.2. Productivity and efficiency in the government-funded health system

Peru has taken several important steps in recent years to improve the productivity and efficiency of SIS. In particular, there has been extensive innovation around payment mechanisms, with results-based financing and, in primary care, capitation-based payments being promising examples. In addition, Service exchange agreements are being used to support integration across SIS, EsSalud and other schemes, and consolidated purchasing of drugs has also worked well.

It is striking, however, how little control SIS has over internal purchasing and redistribution of funds. In many respects, the Ministry of Economy and Finance plays a greater role in determining purchasing and service provision within SIS than MINSA does. It is not clear whether these arrangements are appropriate (in a nominally decentralised system), or sustainable, given the risk of eroding MINSA's capacity for budget-management. Peru should consider, therefore, whether such extensive operational control of SIS's budget by MEF remains appropriate. Greater use of Health Technology Assessment for cost-effectiveness and budget-impact analyses would also be an important step to introduce clearer accountability for spending decisions, and actuarially-based budget allocations.

SIS has innovated extensively around payment mechanisms and service delivery models

Innovations with results-based financing (PpR) appear promising

Over the last decade, the Ministry of Health and Ministry of Economy and Finance (MEF) have introduced new payment mechanisms within SIS to encourage more efficient allocation of resources. In particular, Budgeting for Results Programmes (*Presupuestos por Resultados*, PpR) were started in 2007, in the context of its National Budget System Reform led by MEF. Under this approach, budgeting switched from budget lines (human resources, goods and services, etc.) to a productivity-based approach.

PpR is defined as "a public management strategy that links resource allocation to products and measurable results for the population" (MEF, 2015). Its methodology includes a careful choice of interventions, definition of the expected results and a commitment from participating institutions to achieve them.

PpRs are intended, therefore, to establish public spending accountability, mechanisms for data generation related to outputs or outcomes, and the steps taken to achieve them. In addition, by selecting interventions based on health priorities, PpR is meant to improve allocative efficiency as well as performance. In effect, the allocation of resources translates into a reprioritisation of resources towards the interventions specified in the PpR. PpRs are also a mechanism to mobilise additional resources for selected interventions.

PpRs have been introduced as part of the budgeting system at all government levels. In 2014, 70% of the total government budget for all sectors was allocated through 73 PpR programmes also for all sectors. In 2015 the number of these programmes increased to 85. The health sector is possibly one of the sectors that has made most progress in implementing them, with PpR now present in almost all spheres of activity (Figure 3.5).

Figure 3.5. Health sector financing and budgeting for results

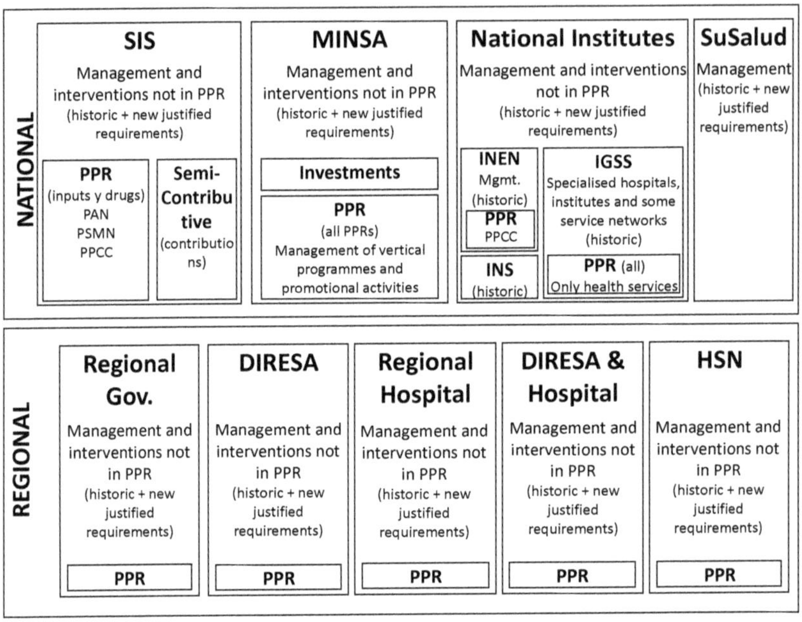

The steps in the PpR budget process, as applied the HIV/AIDS programme by way of illustration, are shown in Table 3.4. All agents participating in the supervision and delivery of services help formulate the budget, including (in this particular example): the HIV/AIDS national programme, the National Centre for Provision of Health Strategic Resources (CENARES), the National Health Institute (INS), SIS, the Health Regional Directorate (DIRESA) and the hospitals.[5] In the second stage, MEF consolidates the information to arrive at a final design for the national scheme. Although there may be adjustments throughout the year in the national scheme, these must be approved by the regional governments and by MEF (the third stage). The monitoring of the PpR programme expenditures is done by relevant specialist agencies, intermediate results are monitored by MEF, the national programme and SIS. Finally, MEF monitors overall achievement.

Table 3.4. Budget process for Peru's HIV/AIDS PpR programme

Stage		MEF	HIV/AIDS National programme	National Centre for Provision of Health Strategic Resources	INS	SIS	Reg. Gov.	DIRESA	Hospitals
1	Formulation and implementation		X	X	X	X		X	X
2	Consolidation	X	X				X		
3	Approval	X					X		
4	Monitoring of expenditures	X	X	X	X	X	X	X	X
5	Monitoring of intermediate results	X	X			X			
6	Monitoring of final results	X							

Note: DIRESA: Health Regional Directorate; INS: National Health Institute; Reg. Gov.: Regional governments.

Source: Vargas, V. (2015), "The New HIV/AIDS Program in Peru: The Role of Prioritizing and Budgeting for Results".

Some evidence of the impact of PpR programmes is available. The Maternal and Neonatal Health PpR includes normal deliveries as one of its outputs. Spending on normal deliveries increased from S/.62.2 million in 2009 (equivalent to USD 20.7 million or EUR 14.8 million) to S/.192.5 million in 2014 (equivalent to USD 67.8 million or EUR 51.1 million). In this same period, the percentage of institutional deliveries (public or private providers) performed by skilled health workers (medical doctor, midwife and nurse) increased from 81.3% to 89.2%, increasing at a higher rate among women living in rural areas (MEF, 2015).

Another example is the Articulated Nutrition Programme, where spending increased from S/.1.052 billion in 2009 (equivalent to USD 349.3 million or EUR 251.1 million) to S/.1.35 billion in 2014 (equivalent to USD 476.3 million or EUR 359.1 million). During this period there was a re-allocation of resources across services, in particular, toward childhood growth and development checks (*Control de Crecimiento y Desarrollo*, CRED, in the table below) and iron supplementation. The PpR programme coincided with a reduction in malnutrition from 23.8% in 2009 to 14.6% in 2014 (among children under five years of age).

PpR clearly have a role in improving health system performance. Nevertheless, their risks should also be considered. In particular, while PpR may improve how budgets are allocated, they do not address the question of total financial resources needed for the health sector. They also risk causing further fragmentation of funding sources, because PpRs are established for specific health problems or population groups. They therefore risk omitting a system-wide view of activity and budgeting. Specifically, PpR programmes remain disconnected from other health benefits packages such as PEAS, FISSAL or the Hope Plan. Because PpRs are disease-specific, they generate a dual budgeting system for SIS: resources under the disease-specific PpRs and, for all other services, resources based on a historic budgeting methodology.

Capitation-based payment in primary care has been introduced to encourage population health management

In 2011, SIS started using capitation to partially pay for primary care services provided by regional governments. One agreement was signed in 2011 (with Huancavelica region), four regions followed in 2012, and the remaining 20 regions signed in 2013. Initially, these agreements only included primary care services provided in health centres and health posts, but were later expanded to include primary care in small hospitals.

SIS introduced capitation payment with the twin goal of incentivising proactive population-based care, as well as speeding up the transfer of funds to the regions. Previously, regional governments had complained about delayed financial transfers from SIS, related to the complexity of the mechanism used. Providers produced a report on the services provided to SIS beneficiaries; then subnational entities (*unidades ejecutoras*) consolidated the information at the subnational level; reports were sent to SIS; SIS sent them back with requests for clarification; and finally SIS paid. It often took more than 6 months to process primary care payments under this process.

Unfortunately, the new agreements fell short in establishing a mechanism to make sure that payments reached clinics more quickly. Furthermore, the intention to incentivise proactive population-based care was also weaker than intended, because capitation payments are allocated to administrative units at regional level, giving them autonomy to decide allocations to health facilities. There is only very limited information on the amount of resources that are channelled through these capitation payments. In the case of Amazonas, a recent study showed that they fluctuated between 1.6% and 10.1% in 2015, with an average of 6.1% of total budget. This suggests that, in general, funding through this mechanism is low.

Service exchange agreements are being used to support integration, but current arrangements risk financial sustainability

A third area for reform concerns service-exchange agreements. Previously, SIS had to buy all services from the government-funded provider network, and EsSalud relied entirely on its own network. This was inefficient as it did not optimise use of all available providers, leading to unmet need or over supply in some cases. To address this issue, Peru has recently allowed contracting across subsystems in an effort to improve efficiency and sustainability by pooling at least some health services.

As a first step in this process, regulations were changed in 2011 to allow SIS to sign service exchange agreements with Lima's Municipality Solidarity Hospitals (*Hospitales de la Solidaridad*, SISOL), not formally part of SIS's provider network.[6] Later, in 2013, regulations were further modified to allow SIS to purchase services from EsSalud providers, and EsSalud to purchase services from public providers. The total amount spent through cross-sector contracts has increased in the last three years, although its share in the total budget still remains almost negligible – around 1% of SIS's total budget. As discussed earlier, SIS beneficiaries are increasingly seeking care from other private providers. Part of this rising demand may be absorbed by the cross-sector agreements.

One of the challenges with these agreements is that the payment mechanisms used risk the financial sustainability of SIS. Specifically, service-exchanges are paid for on a fee-for-service basis that encourages over-provision. Furthermore, government transfers to SIS are calculated on the basis of the variable costs of services (since SIS only controls this element of provider payment), while cross-sector purchases by SIS are priced at full cost. This worrying inconsistency may threaten SIS' financial sustainability if not accompanied by additional resources.

An additional point is that the decision on which interventions to buy from other providers only considers services not being provided *at all* by a given local provider network. It does not consider services that are provided, but subject to high demand. Quality and access could improve if service-exchanges were also expanded to include these services.

Broadly, however, SIS has little control over internal purchasing and redistribution of funds

MEF exercises substantial control over the SIS budget – both in terms of its overall allocation (as discussed in Section 3.1), and its allocation and disposal within SIS. Indeed in key respects, MEF has more influence over how SIS allocates its budget than the Ministry of Health. Changes in primary-care capitation payments to regional governments are dependent on MEF approval, for example, and SIS has previously been blocked from hiring additional health workers.

The extent to which MEF's far-reaching oversight of SIS financing (to the possible exclusion of the Ministry of Health) is justified, is open to question. On the one hand, such oversight may indicate a lack of clear rules on the distribution of roles and functions in Peru's health insurance system, as well as a lack of confidence in the technical capacity of the Ministry of Health. On the other hand, the oversight may provide a stronger framework for accountability and ensuring public value.

MEF's limitation on hiring additional health care workers, may illustrate the latter point. In general, regulations state that human resources should be funded by regional government. However, increased health care demand was not accompanied by additional ear-marked funds from regional governments for this purpose, meaning that, in effect, regional governments were diverting existing funds (originally destined for service provision) to hire additional workers. Although the new budget rule is intended to force regional government to find new funds for health care workers and hire them directly (instead of through SIS), the risk is that the shortage of health care workers will be exacerbated. Once again there is a need for clearer consistency between Peru's pledge to universal health insurance and the necessary resources to implement it.

External purchasing and procurement mechanisms have also improved

SIS has made substantial progress in developing strategic purchasing, as illustrated by three key policies. First, reforms in 2009 and 2013 enabled mechanisms to achieve economies of scale through centralised purchasing of drugs (both generic and on-patent). Second, as discussed earlier, SIS began to buy services from providers outside the public network and, signed agreements with the regional governments to partly finance primary care through capitation rather than pure fee-for-service. Third, efforts have also been made to explicitly define the benefits and to institutionalise health technology assessment (HTA). Whilst successful, there is certainly scope to deepen and extend the reach of these initiatives.

Consolidated purchasing of drugs has worked well in the past, but may now have reached a plateau

MINSA's reforms in the purchasing of essential medicines over the past decade has improved both supply and quality. There are two innovative purchasing mechanisms; one for the national health strategies (HIV/AIDS, tuberculosis, and others) financed by MINSA, and another financed through corporate purchasing. The first mechanism – known as centralised purchasing – is based on the list of drugs directly required by the National

Strategies for particular patient groups. The National Centre for the Supply of Strategic Resources for Health (*Centro Nacional de Abastecimiento de Recursos Estratégicos en Salud*, CENARES) purchases and distributes these drugs.

The second mechanism – known as corporate purchasing – has several stages. First, hospitals, clinics or regional governments that are interested in participating send their annual consumptions to DIGEMID. This institution then consolidates a list of candidate medications provided that i) they are part of the Single National List of Essential Medicines (PNUME) and that the total purchase order for a drug is at least S/. 60 000 (equivalent to USD 18 831 or EUR 16 975). Next, CENARES opens reverse auctions (where a maximum price is set and suppliers compete by underbidding each other) to establish the best prices for predetermined volumes. Finally, each institution or regional government signs the purchasing contracts with the selected providers for the negotiated price and the agreed volume.

In 2016, over 400 medications were purchased in this way. In 2013, corporate purchasing represented 28.4% of MINSA's total drug budget and 29.3% of EsSalud. Prices have decreased substantially: according to an analysis of five key drugs,[7] corporate purchases have reduced prices by 64.8% between 2002 and 2012 (Crisante, 2013). Furthermore, availability of drugs in public entities reached 78.1% by December 2015 (DIGEMID, 2016).[8] Another benefit is that corporate purchasing sector is done for the entire health care system – regional governments, Armed Forces and National Police health systems and EsSalud. This is an important effort to overcome health sector segmentation.

The benefits of the corporate purchasing mechanism may, however, have reached a turning point. First, expensive drugs that are bought in very small quantities are likely to be excluded from the list given the established minimum amount of each order. This is particularly relevant for EsSalud, which finances many high cost treatments. Specifically, EsSalud's corporate purchases represent less than half of their total drug expenditure. Second, the procurement process is a reverse auction. CENARES previously set the maximum price based on the previous year's winning price. Adjustments to this process in 2015 allowed additional factors such as inflation, exchange rates and supplier submissions to be taken into account. Nevertheless, the reverse bidding process may now be limiting the ability of suppliers to participate: in 2015, 72 auctions concluded with a single provider, making the auction less competitive. This means that competition no longer exists for close to 20% of the drugs and many providers have stopped to offer these drugs altogether.

Health Technology Assessment is under-used at national level

Peru has taken some important steps in developing its capacity for health technology assessment. In 2015, EsSalud's Institute for Health Technological Assessment and Research (*Instituto de Evaluación de Tecnologías en Salud e Investigación*, IETSI) started to carry out systematic reviews related to devices, equipment and medications and made some initial cost-effectiveness analyses in 2016. The General Office for Research and Technological Transfer of the National Health Institute (*Instituto Nacional de Salud*, INS) has also carried out several quality HTAs in the past, but this task has been interrupted due to instability in its leadership.

These initiatives indicate Peru's interest to institutionalise the use of HTA in all its health insurers. They are however carried out without co-ordination and thereby replicate the fragmented character of Peru's health system. There are powerful reasons why the institutionalisation of HTA at the national level would benefit the country as a whole: by saving costs and avoiding duplications; by promoting the streamlining of methods and processes; and, by introducing a common denominator of evidence when informing reimbursement decisions for all the segments of Peru's health sector (IADB, 2016).

Decentralisation has complicated SIS's ability to manage risks

As in many other Latin-American countries, Peru made regional decentralisation of government a major policy goal over recent years. The transfer of management of health services and accompanying financial resources to local governments was made in order to improve responsiveness and efficiency. It was thought that decentralisation would lead to greater cost awareness at the local level, which in turn would have a positive effect on technical efficiency. Local decision-makers' knowledge of local circumstances should also allow them to tailor services and spending patterns to local needs and preferences, improving allocative efficiency.

Peru's decentralisation of government began in 2002 with the election of autonomous regional governments. The decentralisation in the health sector was completed between 2004 and 2006. Currently, regional governments manage health services through Regional Health Directorates (*Direcciones Regionales de Salud*, DIRESAS). Exceptionally, MINSA continued to manage the health services in Lima until 2013, when the Health Services Management Institute (*Instituto de Gestión de Servicios de Salud*, IGSS) was created to take over the management of Lima's public providers. Since December 2016, however, MINSA is again the institution responsible for public health provision in the capital.

Health sector decentralisation has been challenging to implement, however, for several reasons. First, the transfer of functions to the subnational levels was not sufficiently planned (as explained further below). Second, central authorities lost substantial power with regards to some key public health and preventive health care activities that are best discharged at national level. Third, co-ordination between central and regional authorities is not always effective. All of these issues suggest lack of clear definition in the national and regional governments' respective roles.

Decentralisation did not establish mechanisms to articulate priorities across different levels of government

The transfer of functions to subnational levels was not based on a thorough assessment of the regional governments' management capacities, particularly in the poorer regions of the country. Furthermore, regional governments did not have the experience to manage health care providers and they received little guidance to do so. According to the Contraloría General (2014), the transfer of functions was not accompanied with all the necessary resources, support for capacity building and supervision and control mechanisms. Lack of transparency and accountability at the regional level was a particular problem and, in some cases, corruption in the regional governments also became a serious concern.

Decentralisation also failed to establish clear mechanisms to articulate and co-ordinate priorities across national and subnational levels. MINSA, for example, was not given mechanisms to perform its role as overall steward of the health system (Francke, 2013). Currently MINSA only co-ordinates the supply of inputs and medicines requested by DIRESAs for their health strategies, with little opportunity for strategic oversight or co-ordination. Although, DIRESA directors hold meetings with the Minister of Health to discuss policy approaches and guidelines, the agreements are not legally binding (Francke, 2013), which leads to a weak commitment to work in line with the policy guidelines.

Failure of key public health programmes illustrates the difficulties of rapid decentralisation

Lack of overall co-ordination has become particularly problematic with regards to the National Health Strategies (Francke, 2013). Prior to the decentralisation reforms, these health strategies used to be MINSA's main operational activities. MINSA is still in charge of designing the National Health Strategies and of centrally purchasing the necessary supplies and medicines, but the actual provision of care is now managed regionally or locally. MINSA, however, has little power to hold regional governments accountable for implementing its policies.

Routine childhood vaccination, an essential public health function, illustrates this situation. In 2009 one regional government received 12 000 vaccines and only 26 children were vaccinated. MINSA did not have a mechanism to hold the local government accountable for the implementation of the vaccination programme. Six years later the judicial process against the regional governor is still ongoing (Comercio, 2015). This same type of problem could arise, for example, in the case of other preventive programmes. Failure of this basic public health function is worrying.

To further aggravate MINSA's lack of control of key public health issues, national programmes are increasingly being linked to the PpRs, managed by MEF, as described earlier. Although PpRs are meant to increase transparency and accountability, the lack of co-ordinated strategic oversight of regional activities (such as should ordinarily be provided by MINSA) risks weakening Peru's public health infrastructure.

3.3. Recommendations to improve the sustainability and efficiency of the government-funded health system

This section considers the steps that Peru should take to ensure effective access to SIS services; use resources efficiently through strategic purchasing; generate sufficient and sustainable resources; and, manage risk and have the tools and resources to do so. Action in each of these areas will ensure that SIS continues to offer high quality, efficient and sustainable health care to the Peruvian population.

Establish a clear roadmap toward fully achieving UHC

First and foremost, attention must be given to extending health insurance to those who remain without formal insurance, principally workers in the informal sector. In order to meet this challenge, there are two possible long-run roles for SIS: either to consolidate as the main insurance option not only for the poor and the vulnerable, but also for the independent/informal workers and for workers in small enterprises who currently have no health coverage; or to shrink as the economy grows and the eligible population for its subsidised regime decreases.

Under the first scenario, the number of individuals affiliated to SIS's semi-contributory schemes would increase (assuming the economy continues to grow), compared to those belonging to the subsidised regime. SIS would need policies that ensure that the informal sector will indeed affiliate to the semi-contributory schemes as their income rises. As discussed earlier, however, previous initiatives to cover this population have not been particularly successful. This may be due to a misunderstanding of what this population seeks in terms of coverage, or choice of provider. They seem to value care from private providers, and have some ability to pay for insurance. Such desire for choice should be taken into account when designing a health insurance plan that non-poor individuals would be willing to purchase. Under this scenario, SIS and EsSalud would persist in segmented system, with the informally employed and the poor belonging to the former, and the formally employed belonging to the latter.

In the second scenario, SIS will focus only on the poor and its role within the health sector will shrink as the economy develops. Just as in the first scenario, however, there would have to be a clear plan to cover those who are no longer poor, specifying how to incentivise or mandate affiliation to a (semi-) contributory scheme. Indeed, whatever the scenario, Peru needs a clear graduation process to absorb the population graduating from fully subsidised insurance, encouraging or mandating them to enrol in a (semi-) contributory scheme. As previously discussed, however, the current AN does not make clear the mechanisms and institutions that will underpin the achievement of UHC in the longer term. If no long-run policies are put in place for a smooth transition from coverage under the subsidised regime to a contributory regime, social unrest could ensue, risking the political sustainability of the entire system.

Looking at other countries' experience in managing this transition, Bitrán (2014) concludes that two strategies have been most successful: either offering a limited benefits package with a low premium for previously fully-subsidised individuals; or, switching from social health insurance to tax-financed system with mandated enrolment. In 2008, for example, China established the health insurance programme (Urban Resident Basic Medical Insurance, URBMI) for informal sector workers.[9] This offered a smaller benefits package compared to the one for formal sector workers, financed through individual contributions and government subsidies (Bitrán, 2014). In 2010, the total premium for URBMI was 8.9% of the total premium for formal sector workers. In terms of benefits, URBMI offered 47.9% inpatient reimbursement rate compare to 68.2% for formal sector workers; URBMI finances outpatient care with out-of-pocket payments and subsidies, while formal sector workers use health savings accounts.

The option of offering reduced coverage at lower cost, however, does not seem feasible in Peru for two reasons: i) a minimum benefits package already exists (PEAS) and it is not small; and ii) Peru's explicit commitment to reaching universal health coverage.

An example of the other alternative, that is switching from social health insurance to tax-financed system with universal enrolment, would be Brazil. Brazil eliminated its segmented system and created the Unified Health System (*Sistema Único de Saúde*, SUS) in 1988. SUS is a tax-financed agency that provides comprehensive health care to all Brazilians. Another example is Indonesia. In 2014, Indonesia reformed its SHI system by establishing a single payer, as well as tax-based financing for workers with an income below a certain threshold.

Incrementally expand SIS's benefit package, ensuring that resources match service obligations

Changing epidemiology, demand, health technologies, cost and prices all demand that a health insurance benefits package continuously evolve. Otherwise, it risks becoming unable to meet people's health care demands and losing legitimacy. Similarly, if financial allocations do not evolve to match service obligations, effective coverage is jeopardised. In short, a benefits package needs to be accompanied by systematic, periodic and technically robust processes to update its scope and funding.

Policies, institutions and mechanisms to regularly and systematically update PEAS, however, are currently lacking in Peru – or at least the responsibility to do so has never been effectively enforced. Correcting this should be a priority. In particular, Peru should review the methodology used to prepare the List of Drugs for National Purchase, including high cost drugs. This will require co-ordination with FISSAL and EsSalud, and so offers an opportunity to better articulate the health system. OECD countries such as the Netherlands, Israel or Estonia have institutionalised processes to systematically update their benefits packages and Peru should look to these and other countries for guidance. More locally, for example, Chile mandates that its benefits package AUGE must be updated regularly, while Colombia stipulates that its benefits package POS is updated every year and that process has to rest on evidence and participatory processes.

It is equally critical that SIS resources are based on actuarial studies of expected need. Greater coherence between financial allocations to SIS and the actuarial cost of PEAS should be technically straightforward, given that the legal framework mandates this alignment. Hence, Peru should take steps to enforce the legal framework (Law 29344, the *Aseguramiento Universal en Salud*) that mandates that the SIS budget should be based on actuarial studies.

A number of accompanying policies, however, will also need to be developed to ensure effective delivery of the benefits package. PEAS still does not have, for example, clinical management guidelines for all the health problems it covers. Developing such guidelines will support the consistent delivery of pathways of care and reduce practice variation.

Achieving equality between the SIS and EsSalud benefits packages should be a priority

The legitimacy of the SIS benefits package is subject to further pressure given the co-existence of other, more generous packages such as that offered by EsSalud. Hence, another objective must be to ensure that the SIS and EsSalud benefits packages (the two most important in Peru) become more equal. Steps in this direction should go hand-in-hand with processes to expand and update PEAS as outlined above.

Other countries with fragmented health systems have taken steps towards equalizing benefits packages across insurers without necessarily moving towards single payer systems. For example, explicit guarantees (AUGE) were adopted in Chile, while the private system (ISAPRES) and the public insurance (FONASA) were maintained. Uruguay created the National Integrated Health System, where multiple Institutions of Collective Medical Attendance (IAMC) coexist with public insurers, offering a common benefits package financed through a common fund.

Colombia has a multi-payer system, but adopted a single benefits package with similar per capita allocations for all residents, and risk equalisation funds to ensure equity in the allocation of resources (Uthoff et al., 2012). Furthermore, in Colombia, health insurers can affiliate persons from both the subsidised and the contributory regimes. Peru should start discussions to develop a strategic plan and technical roadmaps to further integrate its health system, with regards to benefits packages, financing, and the provision of services.

Embedding Health Technology Assessment, through a dedicated agency, should underpin efforts to expand the benefits package

Sustained and efficient expansion of the SIS benefits package should be underpinned by robust health technology assessment (HTA). MINSA should lead the effort of co-ordinating and reinforcing the existing agencies that are starting to carry out HTA in Peru. The activities of IETSI in EsSalud, or the INS and DIGEMID in MINSA, for example, could be coordinated by a umbrella body (and eventually, perhaps, consolidated into a single, national HTA agency). As well as advising on expansion of the SIS benefits package, a system-wide HTA function would be to determine the coverage and price of high cost drugs.

Using HTA to determine what is financed by health systems is increasingly used in several countries in Latin America. Colombia, for example, has constituted an independent national HTA agency, IETS (*Instituto de Evaluación de Tecnologías Sanitarias*) which systematically and routinely provides recommendations to the Ministry of Health on the benefits and costs of health technologies. Likewise, in Uruguay, a National High Cost Drug Fund, FNR (*Fondo Nacional de Recursos*), evaluates new drugs to determine whether they should be provided by it universal health system.

One of the best known HTA institutes is the United Kingdom's NICE (National Institute for Health and Care Excellence, www.nice.org.uk) which appraises health technologies and produces recommendations on whether they should or should not be provided by the national health system. There are multiple institutional models used to institutionalise HTA (IADB, 2016). Whichever the path chosen, it is important that processes are systematic, technically robust, participatory, independent and ideally established at the national level.

Address deficiencies in SIS workforce and infrastructure through functional integration with other provider networks

Given the shortfalls in workforce numbers and bed density discussed earlier, it is clear that sustained investment in Peru's health system infrastructure is necessary. The pace at which Peru reaches parity with regional and international comparators is a decision that will have to be balanced against competing priorities within the overall government investment plan.

In the shorter term, however, there is scope to increase access to health care by overcoming some of the structural barriers that characterise the Peruvian health care system. In particular, functional integration through greater use of service-exchange agreements (allowing SIS affiliates to use EsSalud facilities, or vice versa) is an initiative that should be exploited further. Integrated networks should correspond to geographical areas underpinned by detailed understanding of local population health care needs. Currently the networks only consider public sector providers. Local service networks could also include selected private health care providers. This been successful in countries such as Denmark, Norway, Croatia, the Czech Republic and Hungary.

Again, steps toward further service-exchange agreements should go hand-in-hand with processes to expand and update PEAS, as outlined earlier, aiming toward full equality with the EsSalud (and other insurers') packages. As equity approaches, there will be space to debate offering choice of insurer, irrespective of employment status. In theory, health insurance competition can enhance efficiency in health care administration and delivery, if insurers do not cherry-pick individuals, if insurers are able to influence health service quality and costs, and if transaction costs are kept low (Thomson et al., 2013).

Some countries have chosen to exploit the potentially beneficial impact of health insurer competition in their health systems. For example, Colombia established a universal mandatory health plan and a risk-adjusted per capita payment to promote competition among insurers. Restrepo (2004) finds that insurers' strategies included reforms to improve the quality of services and control costs, associated with their exposure to competition. Peru remains, however, considerably far from this scenario, given the differences across insurers' benefits packages that persist.

Service exchange agreements may open the way to separation of the insurer and purchaser roles

Service-exchange agreements also imply separation, in theory at least, of the provider role from the insurer role within SIS, EsSalud and Peru's other insurer/provider entities. Such separation has the potential to to increase transparency, accountability and efficiency in insurer/provider entities. Interestingly, reforms adopted in 2013 appear to move towards a clearer separation of these roles in Peru. The certification of the Armed Forces and National Police as insurers also hint at the separation between insurers and providers, since to get certification they were required to separate their functions into two different types of institutions, namely insurer and provider.

The benefits or otherwise of separating insurer/provider roles (or, conversely, of integrating them) depend very much on local factors, at a given moment. Integration may allow insurers to more fully control providers' activities and costs; separation may allow providers to compete (on choice and/or quality), and allow patients choice. The degree to which Peru wishes to achieve such separation should be considered carefully. An incremental approach (separating the functions and allowing patient choice for some elements of secondary care, such as elective surgery), in one or more pilot regions, may be a sensible approach, backed by rigorous evaluation of the impacts on health care activities, unmet needs, costs and outcomes.

Within the Americas, several contrasting approaches to this question are evident. Colombia's 1993 health reform implemented a regulated health insurance market (Castaño Yepes, 2004; Restrepo, 2004; Restrepo et al., 2007). As a first step, the Social Security Institute in Colombia was separated into insurers (EPS) and providers (IPS). Second, the regulatory framework stipulates that EPS can allocate up to 30% of their health budgets to their integrated provider networks. A study in 2002, showed that 42% of EPS provided services directly, while the remaining 58% purchased services from other providers (Restrepo, 2004).

In Chile, ISAPRES (private insurers) are not allowed to own health service providers. Copetta (2013) shows that, in spite of its prohibition, ISAPRES were able to maintain vertical ownership of providers through holdings. Yet, the ISAPRES's Association continues to argue in favour of vertical integration with a regulatory framework that promotes the transparency in transfer prices and the promotion of competition (Caviedes, 2013). Similarly, in the United States, Kaiser Permanente, the largest non-profit integrated health care system, self regulates through contracts between the three key entities – the health plan (insurer), medical groups, and hospitals – with incentives to provide high quality, affordable care (Pines et al., 2015).

Improve quality of care at the front line

Another critical task aligned to improving efficiency and sustainability concerns monitoring and improving the quality of care. This is currently carried out mainly by SUSALUD, the National Superintendence of Health. The supervisory role of SUSALUD has grown significantly in recent years and it is now charged with authorizing and monitoring both health insurance funds as well as providers. The fact that SUSALUD is an independent public body is a good basis from which to build quality monitoring and improvement activities, but greater leverage could still be exploited. Two examples illustrate how.

The first concerns how patient feedback is used. Currently, SUSALUD provides two mechanisms to incorporate patient views in its quality control activities: it resolves patient complaints against providers and insurers, and it oversees annual patient satisfaction surveys. These mechanisms are useful but they respond more to a client satisfaction and do not represent a deep examination of the quality of care. A more robust approach would be to define a far-reaching set of quality standards and metrics (with the patient perspective front and centre), applied to all insurers and providers, and independently monitored by SUSALUD. This definition of quality standards should draw on the framework used by OECD countries, set out in Section 2.3.

The second instance concerns accreditation. The supervisory role of SUSALUD has been strengthened with its ability to sanction providers and insurers who fail to meet its standards. This is a promising step. Yet, accreditation could be strengthened still further if SUSALUD were to move away from one-off assurance of minimum standards, toward continuous quality improvement and creation of a culture that underpins this. SUSALUD should look to develop this capacity. Other mechanisms to monitor and improve quality of care are addressed in Chapter 2.

... with a particular focus on strengthening primary care

Primary care has been defined as the entry point of Peru's health system, and important steps have been taken to strengthen primary care within SIS and the other insurers. A wide variety of primary care providers exist: MINSA, for example, has four types of primary care providers and EsSalud another four categories (which do not completely correspond to the SIS categories). Private providers also have an array of providers, from physician offices to all-levels-of-care clinics. Such diversity is not necessarily a problem, and may be entirely appropriate given the territorial diversity of the country. Nevertheless, certain caveats need to be in place for such a diverse system to work well.

First, critical common elements such as clinical guidelines, quality standards and monitoring frameworks should be defined in primary care, irrespective of provider-type. In other words, the primary care service model that Peru develops should be flexible enough to adapt to large differences across regions in terms of need and available resources, whilst being structured enough to guarantee the provision of quality care. This issue is, in theory, addressed through the access and quality guarantees included in PEAS. Not all such guarantees, however, are being effectively implemented. A priority, therefore, must be to ensure implementation of PEAS guarantees to promote quality care within essential benefits package.

Second, patients should be given guidance on the appropriate level type of provider for their health care need. Finally, all primary care providers should be supported to maximize their capacity to resolve patient health care needs. One illustration of these issues concerns prenatal care. Previously, only medical doctors were allowed to provide this; now, however, midwives are also allowed to do so. This flexibility allows for more access (especially in remote regions where trained physicians are scarce), and has been accompanied by clear standards, guidelines and quality indicators to ensure consistently high-quality care.

Continue refinement of payment and procurement mechanisms

Most health systems use a blend of payment mechanisms, to balance the twin priorities of responding to health care needs while containing costs (OECD, 2016b). Capitation payments, for example, are often used in primary care to incentivise preventive services. In contrast, a system of diagnosis-related groups (DRG) often underlies payment for episodes of hospital care, since these help standardize pathways of care and associated costs, whilst protecting patient choice.

Peru is taking steps to diversify and optimize its payment mechanisms, introducing capitation in primary care for example, and ongoing experimentation and refinement should be pursued. In the hospital sector, for example, there is scope for SIS to move away from the fee-for-service mechanism that is currently dominant, towards a DRG mechanism, or payments based on clinical outcomes. The responsibility for designing and managing such innovations should be increasingly shared between MINSA and MEF, and not fall exclusively to MEF as currently occurs.

One of the most positive changes in Peru's procurement capability was the introduction of the centralised purchasing for drugs. But, as mentioned above, it has stopped evolving and it needs to be reassessed. In particular, the reverse auction process should be reviewed to allow for more competition. There may also be gains from expanding the list of manufacturers beyond those provided by WHO (Dongo, 2016). In particular, WHO's list does not include countries that have their own production lines.[10] For example, Brazil produces several vaccines at low-cost. Expanding the list of approved producers could help to further reduce prices and improve efficiency. The expansion of this list should, or course, guarantee medication quality and safety.

Strengthen governance at all levels of the health system

Considerable thought has been given to strengthening governance in Peru over recent years, in health as well as other areas of public policy. Key regulatory functions, for example, have been moved into arm's-length agencies to bolster their independence. Despite these promising steps, there remains considerable scope to strengthen governance in Peru's health sector. Three issues, in particular, are pertinent: first, the capacity of MINSA to provide strategic oversight and regulation for the whole health system; second, the levers given to SIS to fulfil its role as the country's largest health insurer; and third, the division of responsibilities between central and local government.

Turning to the first issue, MINSA, as the country's principal health authority, should provide strategic oversight and regulation of all insurer/provider entities operating within Peru. In recent years, a number of steps have been taken to strengthen this stewardship function. MINSA has been reorganised, for example, by separating key functions into new Vice-ministries; other functions have been strengthened by being moved into semi-independent arm's-length agencies. More could be done, however, to clarify overall leadership within in the health system as a whole. One notable aspect, for example, concerns governance of the other insurer/provider entities beyond SIS. EsSalud depends on the Ministry of Labour, for example, and is not accountable to MINSA. Whilst it is not currently practical, or necessary, to bring EsSalud under the stewardship of MINSA, mechanisms to align all insurer/provider priorities should be developed.

Within the OECD, health systems such as France, the Netherlands, Israel and the Czech Republic have multiple insurer/provider entities. In each case, though, the Ministry of Health has a clear and prominent role in setting national health priorities and holding all insurer/providers to account for delivering them (OECD, 2017b).

SIS needs the tools and capacity to better fulfil its role in managing population health risk and institutional financial risk

In terms of the second issue, SIS's capacity to effectively manage health insurance, it is striking that SIS has little delegated competency to fulfil this role. Critical insurance activities, such as specifying who to insure, what benefits to offer and what services to purchase from which providers, do not fall within SIS's competencies, but are made by MINSA or MEF. Parameters such as who to insure, what benefits to offer and what services to purchase directly impact SIS's ability to meet health care demands responsively and efficiently whilst avoiding overspends – areas for which it retains front-line responsibility.

This misalignment between responsibilities and competencies is an argument, therefore, to consider giving SIS greater leverage in planning and delivering health care insurance. Gradual transformation of SIS into a fully effective insurer will require strengthening its capacity to analyse epidemiological and actuarial data and produce projections of demand and activity. This will enable SIS to be a key player in the design and execution of future expansion in the population and service coverage it provides, on the path to UHC. Expanding SIS competencies and technical capacity, under adequate supervision from MINSA, MEF and other regulatory authorities, will enable it to better manage both population health risk and institutional financial risk. This, in turn, will lead to greater financial sustainability.

Risk management is a critical insurance activity that relates to detailed understanding of the covered population and likely health care needs. Kaiser Permanente, in the United States of America, is a well-known example of an integrated health system based on risk management. Kaiser's information system allows follow-up on individual beneficiaries, rather than just individual episodes of health care, which allows for a thorough analysis of health care needs, activities, costs and outcomes. This also involves implementing the necessary incentives for the staff to maintain good reporting practices, share information on best practices and constantly assess the effectiveness of different procedures.

Better coordination between central and local authorities is needed

Finally, there is an opportunity to strengthen the co-ordination between central authorities (principally SIS and MINSA), and regional authorities, such as regional governments. As discussed earlier, for example, public health activities are currently under the control of regional governments, but MINSA does not any effective mechanism to ensure that they meet priorities set at the national level. A rebalancing of central and regional authority is needed, therefore, to make regional governments more accountable to MINSA for key priorities, whilst retaining ownership of operational decisions. Canada is a good example of a fully federal health system that nevertheless delivers an ambitious and unified national policy agenda; and Australia and Italy are valuable illustrations of the careful re-balancing of central and regional governance (OECD, 2017b).

Ensuring financial sustainability also requires re-balancing central and regional roles. Currently, for example, regions do not have a clear understanding of the cost of delivering services, because such a study has never been undertaken (even at central level). At the same time, though, regions claim they do not have enough funds to deliver care. Considerable clarity could be gained, then, if SIS and MINSA were to improve their costing method, as a basis for regional allocations. Another example concerns regional procurement and supply of medication. Improved methods of stock control, warning regional governments and MINSA when approaching critical stock levels, would reduce the risk of stock out and reduce the need for emergency purchase at higher cost. In each case, there is also a need for regional governments to improve their technical competence around planning, purchasing and providing services.

Develop more comprehensive information systems and use of data

Peru's health system is rich in data, but as noted earlier, the overall information infrastructure remains fragmented. Most information systems are designed from the angle of one particular interest and are poorly integrated. PpR programmes, for example, have information systems which are mainly used to supervise activities and budgeting, without being necessarily linked to data on need from epidemiological surveillance systems. In another example, SIS has developed data infrastructure to monitor activities and payments to providers, which do not always link well with regional governments' information systems on the same measures.

There is also a disconnect between decision-making and research meaning that key policies are not supported by empirical research. MINSA does not have a research department that could provide much needed analysis regarding key policies. Instead, research activities are spread out throughout MINSA's departments. In some cases, there are studies but they have not been made public. For example, the SIS actuarial study was presented at a public conference, but it is still not available to the public or researchers. This lack of transparency hinders in the sustainability of the decision-making process. A more open and coordinated approach to health system research, would benefit several critical policy debates, such as regional resource allocation, the scope of vertical integration, or the expansion of SIS to new population groups.

Further analysis and recommendations to strengthen Peru's information systems on quality of care can be found in the companion publication *Monitoring Health System Performance in Peru: Data and Statistics in Peru* (OECD, 2017).

Conclusions

Peru has taken several important steps to improve the productivity and efficiency of SIS in recent years. Extensive innovation around payment mechanisms, with results-based financing and, in primary care, capitation-based payments are particularly promising examples, alongside service exchange agreements to support integration across SIS, EsSalud and other schemes, and consolidated purchasing of drugs. Nevertheless, Peru's goal to reach universal health coverage by 2021 means that further efficiency gains are crucial, especially in the face of rapidly growing health care demand.

Critical steps that Peru should take to strengthen health system efficiency and sustainability include developing more robust approaches to spending, in particular by continuing to move away from budgets based on historical trends, towards budgeting increasingly based on prioritized outcomes and activities. Greater use of Health Technology Assessment for cost-effectiveness and budget-impact analyses will also be important to introduce clearer accountability for spending decisions, and actuarially-based budget allocations, particularly for pharmaceuticals. One important underlying consideration concerns SIS's ability to manage its income streams and service obligations. Currently, the Ministry of Economy and Finance plays a greater role in determining purchasing and service provision within SIS than MINSA does. These arrangements should be reconsidered, to strengthen capacity within both MINSA and SIS for strategic planning and operational management of health services.

Notes

1. Individuals and families were required to pay for coverage, a fixed premium and families with income higher than a ceiling were not eligible.
2. In Peru, the implementation of laws requires the passing of a Supreme Decree with the implementation rules something that has never been done for the Law of Public Financing.
3. Transfers refer only to payments made for services, it does not include administrative or management expenses.
4. There are also differences within Peru where 12 of the 25 departments have the hospital beds indicator below the national average.
5. The HIV/AIDS national programme is in charge of the strategic planning for all activities at all government levels. CENARES purchases all drugs for the programme. INS is responsible for all testing results. SIS provides coverage for preventive and curative services included in the programme. DIRESAs pay fixed cost like human resources and maintenance of infrastructure and equipment. Hospitals provide health services and testing.
6. SISOL Hospitals are a mixed system: infrastructure is public (owned by some municipalities, not regions or MINSA) and management is private.
7. Amoxicillin 500 mg, captopril 25mg, dicloxacillin 500 mg, metronidazole 500 mg, prednisone 5 mg.
8. The average availability is measured as the percent in stock of a group of prioritised drugs, which include those: directly purchased by users, required for SIS coverage, selected health interventions and birth.
9. The eligible population includes: children, students, elderly without previous employment, migrants in some cities and informal sector workers.
10. WHO Prequalification of Medicines Programme (PQP) helps "ensure that medicines supplied by procurement agencies meet acceptable standards of quality, safety and efficacy" (WHO-Prequal, 2016). The process for manufacturers to include their products in this list is led by WHO. For more information, see: http://www.who.int/mediacentre/factsheets/fs278/en/.

References

Bambarén, C.V. and M.d.S. Alatrista (2015), "Hacia una infraestructura del sector salud con calidad y seguridad para todos los peruanos en el siglo XXI", Paper presented at the III Conferencia Académica, Lima,

Beteta, E. (2014), "Evaluación de los convenios de gestión para la transferencia capitada del SIS a las regiones", Policy Note, World Bank, Lima.

Bitrán, R. (2014), "Universal Health Coverage and the Challenge of Informal Employment: Lessons from Developing Countries".

Castaño Yepes, R.A. (2004), "Integración vertical entre empresas promotoras de salud e instituciones prestadoras de servicios de salud", *Rev. gerenc. políticas salud*, Vol. 3(6), pp. 35-51.

Caviedes, R. (2013), "Integración vertical en salud", http://www.elmostrador.cl/noticias/opinion/2013/01/25/integracion-vertical-en-salud/.

Comercio, E. (2015), "Nuestro sistema descentralizado de salud causa problemas", Interview. El Comercio", http://elcomercio.pe/politica/gobierno/anibal-descentralizado-nuestro-sistema-descentralizado-salud-causa-problemas-noticia-1811435.

Contraloría General (2014), "Estudio del proceso de descentralización en el Perú", Contraloría General de la República, Lima, Peru.

Copetta, C.M. (2013), "Prestadores de Salud, Isapres y Holdings ¿Relación Estrecha?", Superintendencia de Salud, Santiago, Chile.

Crisante, M. (2013), "Mercado farmacéutico y acceso a medicamentos en el Perú", Paper presented at the Reunión Técnica El Derecho a la salud y la investigación clínica, Lima. http://www.paho.org/per/index.php?option=com_content&view=article&id=2389:el-derecho-salud-investigacion-clinica-tema-tratado-reunion-tecnica-ops-oms&Itemid=650.

Curioso, W.H. (2014), "eSalud en Perú: Implementación de políticas para el fortalecimiento de sistemas de información en salud", *Panamerican Journal of Public Health*, Vol. 35(5/6), pp. 437-441

Curioso, W.H., K. Pardo and M. Loayza (2013), "Transformando el sistema de información de nacimientos en el Perú", *Rev Peru Med Exp Salud Publica*, Vol. 30(2), pp. 303-307.

DIGEMID – Dirección General de Medicamentos, Insumos y Drogas (2016), "Evaluación de indicadores de disponibilidad de medicamentos a nivel nacional", DIGEMID, Lima, Diciembre 2015.

Dongo, V. (2016), "Personal interview: Director del Instituto de Evaluación de Tecnologías en Salud e Investigación de EsSalud".

El Comercio (2015a), "Presupuesto del SIS requiere aumentar en 240% en cinco años", *El Comercio*, 28/05/2015, retrieved from http://elcomercio.pe/economia/peru/presupuesto-sis-requiere-crecer-240-cinco-anos-noticia-1814458.

El Comercio (2015b), "Salud en el Perú: acuerdan meta de 170 hospitales estratégicos", *El Comercio*, retrieved from http://elcomercio.pe/peru/pais/salud-peru-acuerdan-meta-170-hospitales-estrategicos-noticia-1818575.

Francke, P. (2013), "Perú: El Sistema Integral de Salud y los nuevos retos para la cobertura universal", World Bank, Washington DC.

Glassman, A. et al. (2016), "Defining a Health Benefits Package: What Are the Necessary Processes?", *Health Systems & Reform*, Vol. 2(1), p. 11, http://dx.doi.org/10.1080/23288604.2016.1124171.

IADB – Inter-American Development Bank (2016), "Interrogantes claves a la hora de diseñar un ente de evaluación de tecnologías sanitarias: Respuestas desde tres perspectivas", Serie de políticas y métodos basados en presentaciones a expertos. Basado en el taller de trabajo organizado en Costa Rica en noviembre de 2015 sobre Institucionalización de la ETS, IADB-CRITERIA, Washington, DC.

MEF – Ministerio de Economía y Finanzas (2015), "¿Qué es Presupuesto por Resultados (PpR)? ", retrieved from http://www.mef.gob.pe/index.php?option=com_content&view=article&id=2122&.

MINSA – Ministerio de Salud (2015), "Información de Recursos Humanos en el Sector Salud: Perú 2014", retrieved from http://observatorio.inforhus.gob.pe/publicaciones/bibliograficos/libro21/polifoliar_2014.pdf.

MINSA/DGGRHS (2013), "Segunda Medición de las Metas Regionales de Recursos Humanos para la Salud, Perú 2007-2015", Ministry of Health, Lima, Peru.

Mokate, K.M. (2001), "Eficacia, eficiencia, equidad y sostenibilidad: ¿Qué queremos decir?", *Series Documentos de Trabajo I-24*, Banco Interamericano de Desarrollo, Washington.

OECD (2017), *Monitoring Health System Performance in Peru: Data and Statistics,* OECD Publishing, Paris, http://dx.doi.org/10.1787/9789264282988-en.

OECD (2017b), *Caring for Quality in Health: Lessons Learnt from 15 Reviews of Health Care Quality*, OECD Publishing, Paris, http://dx.doi.org/10.1787/9789264267787-en.

OECD.Stat. (2016), "OECD.Stat", retrieved from http://stats.oecd.org/.

OECD.Stat. (2016b), Better Ways to Pay for Health Care*, OECD Publishing,* Paris. http://dx.doi.org/10.1787/9789264258211-en

Organización Panamericana de la Salud (2007) "Salud en las Americas", Pan American Health Organization, Washington, DC.

PAHO (2005), "Toronto Call to Action: 2006-2015 Towards a decade of Human Resources in Health for the Americas", Paper presented at the Regional Meeting of the Observatory of Human Resources in Health, Toronto.

Pines, J. et al. (2015), "Kaiser Permanente – California: A Model for Integrated Care for the Ill and Injured", retrieved from http://www.brookings.edu/research/papers/2015/05/04-emergency-medicine-case-studies-medtalk.

Prieto, L., C. Cid and V. Montañez (2014), "Perú: el plan Esencial de Aseguramiento en Salud", in U. Giedion, I. Tristao and R. Bitrán (eds.), *Planes de beneficios en salud de América Latina Una comparación regional*, IADB, Washington, DC.

Restrepo, J.H. (2004), "¿ Qué enseña la reforma colombiana sobre los mercados de salud? ", *Gerencia y Políticas de Salud*, Vol. 3(6).

Restrepo, J.H., J.F. Lopera and S.M. Rodríguez (2007), "La integración vertical en el sistema de salud colombiano", *Revista de Economía Institucional*, Vol. 9(17).

Seinfeld, J. and V.A. Montañez (2012), "Salud La investigación económica y social en el Perú: Balance 2007-2011 y agenda 2012-2016", CIES, Lima.

SIS – Seguro Integral de Salud (2016), "Boletín Estadístico Seguro Integral de Salud", retrieved 15/04/2016, Seguro Integral de Salud, Ministry of Health, Lima, Peru.

SIS (2015a), "Boletín Estadístico Seguro Integral de Salud", SIS.

SIS (2015b), "Estudio financiero actuarial del Seguro Subsidiado, Semisubsidiado y Semicontributivo del Seguro Integral de Salud". Seguro Integral de Salud, Ministry of Health, Lima, Peru.

Thomson, S. et al. (2013), "Statutory Health Insurance Competition in Europe: A Four-country Comparison", *Health Policy*, Vol. 109(3), pp. 209-225.

Uthoff, A., J.M. Sánchez and R. Campusano (2012), "The Health Insurance Market: Lessons on the Conflict between Equivalence and Solidarity", Revista CEPAL(108), retrieved from http://repositorio.cepal.org/handle/11362/11608.

Vargas, V. (2015), "The New HIV/AIDS Program in Peru: The Role of Prioritizing and Budgeting for Results".

WHO – World Health Organization (2006), *The World Health Report 2006: Working Together for Health*, World Health Organization, Geneva.

WHO (2000), *The World Health Report 2000: Health Systems: Improving Performance*, World Health Organization, Geneva.

WHO-Prequal (2016), "WHO – Health Systems and Services: Prequalification of Medicines Programme", retrieved from http://apps.who.int/prequal/.

World Bank (2016), "World Development Indicators", retrieved from: http://databank.worldbank.org/data/reports.aspx?source=world-development-indicators.

Xu, K. et al. (2010), "Exploring the Thresholds of Health Expenditure for Protection Against Financial Risk", retrieved from http://www.who.int/healthsystems/topics/financing/healthreport/19THE-thresv2.pdf?ua=1.

ORGANISATION FOR ECONOMIC CO-OPERATION AND DEVELOPMENT

The OECD is a unique forum where governments work together to address the economic, social and environmental challenges of globalisation. The OECD is also at the forefront of efforts to understand and to help governments respond to new developments and concerns, such as corporate governance, the information economy and the challenges of an ageing population. The Organisation provides a setting where governments can compare policy experiences, seek answers to common problems, identify good practice and work to co-ordinate domestic and international policies.

The OECD member countries are: Australia, Austria, Belgium, Canada, Chile, the Czech Republic, Denmark, Estonia, Finland, France, Germany, Greece, Hungary, Iceland, Ireland, Israel, Italy, Japan, Korea, Latvia, Luxembourg, Mexico, the Netherlands, New Zealand, Norway, Poland, Portugal, the Slovak Republic, Slovenia, Spain, Sweden, Switzerland, Turkey, the United Kingdom and the United States. The European Union takes part in the work of the OECD.

OECD Publishing disseminates widely the results of the Organisation's statistics gathering and research on economic, social and environmental issues, as well as the conventions, guidelines and standards agreed by its members.

OECD PUBLISHING, 2, rue André-Pascal, 75775 PARIS CEDEX 16
(81 2017 36 1 P) ISBN 978-92-64-28272-8 – 2017